SEEING

SPELLS

ACHIEVING

OLIVE HICKMOTT

ANDREW BENDEFY

A New Perspectives Book

ISBN 1904312209 ISBN13 9781904312208
First published in 2006
© Copyright 2006

Olive Hickmott and Andrew Bendefy

Published in the UK by MX Publishing, 335 Princess Park Manor, Royal Drive, London, N11 3GX.
www.mx-publishing.co.uk

Dedication

We would like to dedicate this book to those children, and many adults, who were so confident and bright until they met words.

They may just struggle to read, write or spell the way the rest of us adults think they should.

Let us not let them down any longer but help them to learn the freedom that comes with being able to read and write and hence dramatically increase their self esteem and....enjoy the beauty of language.

To my mother who in her life guided me and since her passing influences me.

Andrew

About the authors

Olive Hickmott is an NLP Master Practitioner and certified coach working with individuals and corporations to enable personal growth, in many aspects of their lives. In corporate life, which she left in 1990, she was an engineering director. She founded her own business and is director of the Hickmott Partnership. Her passion is for enabling people to achieve their goals in any aspect of their lives, especially their health. She

 says it is just a privilege to see what individuals can achieve, when they realise how their mind, body and spirit are all interlinked; so they can decide just how they want to be.

Andrew Bendefy is a Certified Hypnotherapist, NLP Master, Certified Coach and a Master Practitioner in Group Mastery and Dynamics.

 He also owns the company, 'Invest Inside Yourself', involved in working with private clients, companies and those in the educational field. His expertise covers personal health right through to business strategy, training and executive coaching. Andrew's early career was invested as a Buyer for a national UK department store group and later as a European Business Manager for Xerox Ltd.

Acknowledgements

There are many people we wish to thank for their help and influence in writing this book. In particular:

The British Dyslexia Association for collecting and publishing the names of so may well known people with dyslexia; and to the individuals for letting their names be published. This is such an inspiration to those with whom we work.

Ian McDermott, Robert Dilts, Tim Hallbom and Suzi Smith for the ideas and thinking that have contributed much to the authors' ability to write this book.

Peter King, who has inspired so many to realise that with curiosity major changes become possible and the impossible melts away.

St. Luke's School, Redbourn for the enthusiasm and commitment that their staff, pupils and parents have shown.

Peta Gunson, for stoically editing this book through its various iterations and for her valuable input.

Steve Emecz, our interface with the publisher, whose expert advice for the project has been so valuable.

The research and work we have done, for this book, result from inspiring collaborations between Olive Hickmott and Andrew Bendefy. We have relied very much on each another to challenge our thinking and through this process help so many individuals achieve what they have wanted.

Thanks to all the participants at our "Spelling and Reading through 'Visualisation' " seminars who have helped us develop and articulate this approach and without whose valuable assistance, this would not have been possible.

And finally to thank our families who not only read parts of the script but challenged our thinking and above all supported us throughout the project.

The extracts on pages 53 and 83 are from *Rediscover the Joy of Learning* by Don Blackerby (Success Skills Inc, 1996); the extract on page 60 and 113 are from *The gift of Dyslexia* by Ronald Davis (Ability Workshop Press 1994); the extract on page 24 is from *A boy beyond reach* by Dr. Cheri Florance (Simon & Schuster, 2004); the extract on page 29 is from *How Children Learn* by John Holt (Penguin Books 1970)

NEW PERSPECTIVES

With every new day you have a choice, a choice to do things differently.

If you choose the same actions as yesterday, you will get the same results - try another way.

Part 1: Inspirations for change

We all have an invaluable skill

Part 2: Beliefs

Check out what you believe about your own spelling and reading and make sure you are not standing in your own way with limiting beliefs.

Part 3: 'Visualision'

Enhance your essential skill of 'Visualisation' which you already possess; then use the skill for holding words

Part 4: How to overcome 'bewildering'

Reduce and hopefully eliminate, 'bewildering' through a little self discovery and by gaining insights in to how your mind processes new things. Find a new perspective.

Part 5: The sky's the limit

Look ahead to what you might now be able to achieve with this new skill

Preface

By Olive Hickmott

We do the best we can, given the choices we believe are available to us

If I had been born later I would have been labelled dyslexic, but the term was not commonly used in my generation. Instead I feel privileged not to have been given this label, although I knew that my ability to read and spell was well below average.

I struggled through school with lists of words to learn and had poor test results. I don't recall ever trying to read books for pleasure; I had put this down to there not being many books around after World War 2 and those that were had few pictures and no colour. Whenever the class read aloud I felt that it would be best to sink under the desk unnoticed, hoping that the ground would open up and swallow me before my turn came. My turn for what? Just to read a little out of the book we were studying. Not so difficult for most of the class, but hell for me. I was often left until nearly last in the room and I can remember hoping that the bell would ring to end the lesson before it was my turn. Looking back, the teachers were probably being kind, leaving me until later, and sometimes, I escaped without reading, but it did mean the agony was prolonged even longer. When I did read, I would stumble around the words on the page in front of me until the teacher eventually ended my self humiliation. I can't remember being teased by my classmates but goodness knows how I got away with that.

I recall being told by teachers that I thought too quickly to spell correctly and the only response I got when I passed GCSE English was "how did you manage that?" I didn't care about the insult because I was free of those lessons. My spelling gradually improved over the years, and I have to admit to being saved by the 'spell-checker' on my computer, which puts those nice red wavy lines under words and kindly corrects them with just a click of the mouse.

This struggle with English controlled my career. I took Maths at A level and at University, and when people commented on how clever I was, I knew that I actually had no option, for my English, especially my spelling, was too poor for any other subject.

This struggle also meant that I never read for pleasure until I was nearly 40. How could I contemplate reading anything for pleasure when I found it such a nightmare? I also found it extremely difficult to remember what I had read and, when putting a book down, a bookmark was essential. I seemed unable to remember the content of the book which, at the time, I assumed to be my mind wandering on to other things. I studied French for years and never managed to achieve 'O' level – now whose idea was it to teach me another language, when I couldn't spell in my 1st language?

I started work as a computer programmer, never realising that my intuitive understanding of how things work, combined with the logical training of a mathematician was a winning combination for debugging software; I also didn't have to read much. Having progressed into management it wasn't surprising that I focused on developing people rather than reading or creating copious reports.

It wasn't until I attended a Neurolinguistic Practitioner Training Programme (NLP) from International Training Seminars (ITS) that I solved the puzzle. In just 15 minutes Ian McDermott introduced us to a spelling technique I call 'Visual Spelling' that had been developed many years before by understanding how good spellers spell, and then teaching the same technique to those who struggle. It was just a simple demonstration of how our eye movements reflect the activity of our brain, and how NLP assists us to model excellence. For me it was a eureka moment - "why didn't anyone ever tell me that this was how you were expected to spell?" It was also one of those things I didn't know, I didn't know. I had suddenly found the all important 'how to' that had been missing from my life.

Those 15 minutes set me off on this new journey of discovery.

Firstly I had to learn how to teach myself and others how to visualise, and then how to use the same technique for visualising words. But for some of the people I worked with this was nowhere near enough. I needed to help them resolve areas of confusion, such as letters jumping around the page, before they could achieve what they wanted.

As my journey progressed I realised that I could overcome some of the challenges I assumed I had no control over and that, the process of change was really enjoyable.

I realised that the gift I had been given, that confused my reading and spelling, has also been of enormous value. "How does that work?" I hear you ask. We will explain this later. For now, just consider whether you too may have a skill that enables you to see many different perspectives and make extraordinary connections at high speed. In my case, I had taken this skill for granted and not realised that it wasn't second nature for everyone. This skill is invaluable to me and I use it many times a day, every day, especially when coaching individuals and teams. I am now very appreciative of such a valuable gift.

From the Authors

We have written this book to share with others information that has been effective for those we have worked with.

We offer the contents as ideas that may help you make progress towards your goals. It is not intended as a definitive work, as there is always more to learn about self awareness, but we believe it will provide valuable new perspectives for you to start your own personal journeys. The effort you want to put into making these changes is your choice alone.

Many children and adults, have achieved stunning results very quickly, as they discover their missing 'how to's'. The more you put in and understand yourself the faster you will progress. It is not unusual to acquire this new 'how to' in a very short period of time and some have achieved it in less than an hour. It appears that once your brain gets hold of an easier way with words, it is so pleased that it rushes headlong, into this new world; improving your ability to spell and read, and with it your self-esteem and confidence. From those we have

.

encountered, it also seems that confusion over reading and writing is not dependent on IQ levels, but simply masks your ability to reach your true potential.

We hope this book will enable your journey of self-exploration and achievement, enjoying the freedom that comes from reading and writing.

The book is based on working with people and documenting experiences we have seen to work, rather than theoretical principals. You are provided with background information and invaluable tools to help you move forward.

We would appreciate you letting us know your experience so that we can further refine the material presented here. Any valuable further information we come across or develop will be posted on our web-sites.

We have included a few priceless anecdotes to give you a flavour of what individuals have achieved. The names have been changed or they are unattributed to protect anonymity.

Seeing Spells Achieving is one of a series of books about personal development and growth, entitled New Perspectives. They are all focused on inspiring you to achieve the growth you want from within yourself.

We trust you will enjoy this book and let it help you achieve your aspirations.

It never ceases to thrill us, just what individuals can achieve to improve this basic skill. For us it has been a privilege and a discovery to witness people's ability to change so quickly.

Olive Hickmott and Andrew Bendefy

How to use this book

We don't know what we can achieve until we try

Over the last few years we have met hundreds of individuals, who find being able to deal with words really difficult.

This book gives you some tools that will enable you to find dealing with words much easier. Our mission is to help as many individuals as possible develop these skills, in any language, and have the option to reach their potential.

We have made it as easy to read as possible, in an attempt to get this information out to a wide audience. Each section builds on the one before, to assist those with little personal development experience and the pace increases as the book progresses.

You will maximise the benefit of this book if you, or someone who intends to help you, reads it through from the beginning, rather than dipping in and out of the parts that interest you.

The target audience

This book is about change, change for you when dealing with words. The target audience is those who struggle with words themselves and those who work with individuals such as their children or pupils who experience difficulties with words. You don't need to be a trained expert to help yourself or someone else through these simple steps for change.

Those we have worked with are certainly more in control of their symptoms or have eradicated them altogether.

All the necessary information is given in this book and if you would like further assistance you can contact the authors (details can be found at the back of the book) or attend one of our regional training sessions, if you plan to help others on a regular basis.

Individuals who have all sorts of learning difficulties have benefited from this approach. It is for you to determine how much it can assist you.

Further assistance

We have a number of ways that we can further assist our readers.

In order to promote and accelerate the work further Andrew and Olive now offer Seeing Spells Achieving services through their respective practices. This enables them to add other skills from their practices to further extend the services they are able to offer clients.

Please contact them and take a look at their new informative web-sites:

Olive can be contacted through
www.empoweringlearning.co.uk
olive@empoweringlearning.co.uk

Andrew can be contacted through
www.investinsideyourself.com
andrew@investinsideyourself.com

Structure - practices and pictures

There are a number of practices for you to do as you work through the book. These will deepen your understanding.

Pictures are used to illustrate the text. We encourage you to look at the pictures, in the appropriate context, and identify what those pictures means to you. By doing this you will find that your memory and understanding of the text is enhanced – it is a great way of opening up a shift in your thinking.

Working with you and others

All you need is an open mind

In this section you will find a mind mapping chart that walks you through how you would typically improve your skills or work with someone to help them achieve what they want from this book. You read a chart starting at 12 o'clock and then going clockwise around the face.

If you are interested in working to help others we run a training programme to teach 'Seeing spells achieving' in more detail, to train individuals to become "certified practitioners". There are more details of this on the web-site.

Understanding yourself – what are the challenges you have?

Part 1 asks you to be curious about what is going on when you struggle with words, in either spelling, writing or reading and think forward to what success for you and others might be like.

When working with others it is important to understand how they currently achieve what they do before starting to help them visualise words and make their world so much easier. If you are reading this book to change your own abilities, do take time to become clear about how you achieve what you already do. You will find questions in Appendix 2 that may help you achieve that focus.

We also take a look at what may have lead you to being confused with words but also given you an exceptional gift of easily seeing different perspectives. You will realise the potential downsides for words but also the benefits for other things.

What would be the benefit of changing this experience?

Looking forward think in detail about how it will be when dealing with words is a lot easier and what will motivate you to change. What do you want to improve? We suggest you take some time over realising what change will be like for you.

Are you standing in your own way of success?

In Part 2 you think through your beliefs about your own spelling and reading and make sure you are not limiting yourself. You will be encouraged to take ownership for the changes you can make and see where they lead you – we don't know what we can achieve until we try.

Can you visualise?

According to the British Dyslexia Association around 4% (approx 2.5M) of the population is severely dyslexic. A further 6% (approx 3.7M) have mild or moderate problems. In our experience, 100% of those who struggle with words don't use their powers of 'Visualisation' to see words.

Part 3 teaches you to enhance your essential skill of 'Visualisation', which everyone possesses. You need to do this first and make sure it is working for you. Then you will progress to use this skill for holding words – called 'Visual Spelling', to give you a new tool for reading and spelling, one which others take for granted. If you are struggling with words, give yourself permission to use this new tool. Simply have an open mind and see what happens, you may well get the results you want.

If this proves difficult, practise a little and if you are confused, you may like to jump forward to Part 4 and return here later to really understand 'Visual Spelling'.

How to overcome 'bewildering'

Part 4 is for those of you who may still difficulty or 'confusion' with words. Think of it simply as interference to your learning, understandably built up after repeatedly trying hard to succeed and ending up in frustration or 'bewildering'.

The step by step process will guide you through a little self-discovery to gain insights as to how your mind processes new words. You will learn how to develop your own process which feels right for you and works best for you, and can reduce and eliminate the confusion and 'bewildering'. From this new perspective you are now ready to handle words with calm and success in an amazingly short period of time.

What can you achieve now?

Part 5, entitled 'the sky's the limit' does just that, showing you what you can achieve with this new skill. It includes techniques to become a really fast reader now you have the basics in place and describes a technique called mind mapping, which is an invaluable way of taking notes and assembling your thoughts on paper. If you are interested in learning more Tony Buzan has pioneered this work and written several books (see bibliography).

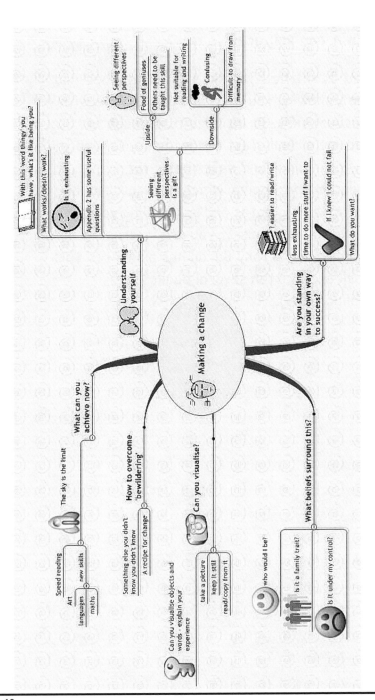

Part 1

Inspirations for change

Dealing with words can be a lot easier - we all have an invaluable skill.

What would success be like?

We all have all the resources we need, or know how to go about finding them.

So what is this secret ingredient for success? It is the power to visualise - and you have it.

The power to visualise is essential and, the great news is that, everyone of us has it !

Before you say "Oh no I haven't", try this.

Would you recognise your parents, friends or colleagues if they walked into the room? And how do you do that?

Somewhere in your memory you have stored an image, a visual picture of each of these people and when you see them you are able to match up what you see with your internal image and recognise the person. If you are at school and some one new joins your class you are immediately able to distinguish them from the others.

Well, visualising words is exactly the same. When you spell and read, you want to be able to access your image or picture that fits with the word you are trying to spell or read.

At school when you were learning to read and spell what would it have been like if you knew you could not fail? Imagine if you knew you already possessed so many skills to enable you to spell and read with ease. How would your world have been different?

Even if you struggle with spelling you are already able to visualise – everyone can. You know what your parents, children or other loved ones look like by recalling a visual picture – we have referred to this ability to recall as 'Visualisation'. It is the way expert spellers excel, in any language. 'Visualisation' is the key that many people have sought over the years; the essential 'how to' remember words. It not only improves your spelling but your reading too. And it is something you already have.

This book is designed to help you develop your 'Visualisation' and other 'how to' skills in a fun and different way. All you need is an open mind and the belief that you will be a better speller or reader; with the right 'how to'.

In this book, you will be introduced to things that you didn't know you didn't know, and that people, who can read or spell well, normally take for granted.

We encourage you to literally take a new look at your reading and spelling difficulties. Strangely enough the skill of 'taking another perspective', or even several, is a natural reaction of those who struggle with reading and spelling, as you will see later.

In fact it can be responsible for difficulties that many of us experience, in one or more of these day to day activities, such as:-

- Reading
- Writing
- Spelling
- Maths, especially symbols. And without symbols maths is quite meaningless
- Understanding and remembering the meaning of what you have read
- Learning mathematical times tables
- Telling the time on a normal clock with hands (non-digital clock)
- Learning a foreign language
- Drawing from memory
- Remembering lists
- Expressing ideas in writing

- Reading music
- Being unsure of whether you are right or left handed
- Taking notes.

We will use the term 'bewildering' to encompass the symptoms that arise from these difficulties. Apologies for corrupting the English language, to write 'bewildering' rather than being 'bewildered', but it's in a good cause. We do this because bewildered is a stuck state, from which it is difficult to progress. For example, when you learnt to walk that must have been very confusing, but if you had sat there 'bewildered' you would have got nowhere. Eventually with lots of persistence, practise, learning from experience, encouragement and the important examples of seeing other children and adults walking, you managed to succeed. 'Bewildering', on the other hand, is a dynamic fluid state and hence it is possible to stop 'bewildering'.

This book is about helping you out of your 'bewildering'. It will help you develop insights to improve your skills, and hence your self esteem.

Whilst you may struggle with either reading or spelling, it is important to remember why you want to do these things. It is in order to communicate with other people. The skills you actually need are reading and writing well enough to be able to successfully communicate, in whatever language is appropriate; you don't need perfection.

If you have been diagnosed with dyslexia you will know that your dyslexia is probably different from the next person's and you will have your own set of difficulties. Again, it is particularly important how you think about and describe your dyslexia to your subconscious mind and once you have a label it is difficult to escape from it. If you say "I am Dyslexic", it is a very stuck state and relates to your very identity. In *A boy beyond reach*, Cheri Florance describes her horror of labelling her son. "I was afraid that if anyone started referring to him as ....handicapped, learning disabled.....or anything, he'd be stuck with that definition........I wouldn't label him, I would talk about what wasn't working."

More accurately and correctly, if you use the terms dyslexia or dyslexic tendencies, this clarifies them as behaviours - what you do, rather than who you are. Other behaviours such as being bored, upset, angry or annoyed are easier to change and you definitely do not plan to remain stuck in one of these states for the rest of your life. Literally translated dys_lexia is "difficulty with language" and if you a have difficulty with something you expect to be able to overcome it. This self talk may sound trivial but it is so important for the way you think about yourself, and will in turn empower your beliefs.

A gift to be treasured

"How do you value yourself?"

It is important to appreciate that having the skill of 'taking different perspectives' is a gift to be treasured.

The ability to manipulate perspectives has enormous value. When a child spontaneously works out this skill for themselves at a young age, they become an expert for the rest of their lives.

It seems peculiar that many children with dyslexic tendencies, or traits, are in special needs schools, when they have a skill that we spend years trying to teach to others.

Parents have frequently reported their child being very bright until it came to words, and then they seemed to stumble. Even in the British Medical Journal as far back as 1896, Dr Pringle Morgan described dyslexia as it is more or less accepted today - "an inability to read occurring in an otherwise bright and developmentally normal child".

Many famous people have had this gift of dyslexia and may have been successful because of it. A fuller list of famous names is available from the British Dyslexic Association web-site.

Hans Christian Anderson	Duncan Goodhew
Alexander Graham Bell	Susan Hampshire
Denis Bergkamp	Goldie Hawn
Marlon Brando	Michael Heseltine
Richard Branson	Damien Hill
Cher	Jeremy Irons
Agatha Christie	Lynda La Plante
Winston Churchill	Jamie Oliver
Tom Cruise	General Patton
Charles Darwin	Steve Redgrave
Leonardo da Vinci	Richard Rogers
Walt Disney	Jackie Stewart
Thomas Eddison	Anthea Turner
Albert Einstein	W. B. Yates
Whoopi Goldberg	Benjamin Zephaniah

The skills that this gift has presented people with include:

- Seeing other people's point of view
- Thinking through a complex operation before starting it
- Holding a picture of how a painting will turn out in their 'mind's eye'
- Not minding being different

- Making things happen through exceptional contributions to the world
- Being very curious - often questioning things that others don't and showing them a better way
- Thinking mainly in pictures, 'Visualisation'
- Thinking for themselves and questioning the status quo
- Being highly intuitive and perceptive
- Having vivid imaginations
- Having above average intelligence
- Visualising things in a creative or different way.

Have people developed some of these other skills because they are not great at spelling and reading, or is it a result of the way they naturally think? What skills have you developed because you are able to see other perspectives?

Making changes

What's the benefit of you changing?

It is most important to feel relaxed when learning to read. John Holt's book '*How Children Learn*', is a real insight to help you understand 'from the child's point of view'. He explains, "I am sure that children as young as two or three, know all too well how little they know, or understand, or can do...........This awareness is very often frightening and humiliating." This covers many of the skills we all need for life, and a quote that will resonate with many is "Most of the time, most of us do not like to be confronted with someone who knows a great deal more about something than we do".

With young children it is essential that they stay relaxed and are not pressurised, using pictures to aid their understanding as much as possible. Above all reading should be fun.

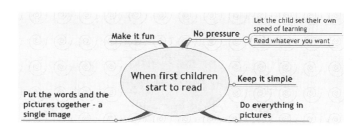

We all learn better when we are in a happy and relaxed state and the same is true for learning to read and write.

When working with older children and adults who, have cleared their 'bewildering', it is normally better for them to choose how they want to improve their reading. Invariably it's not about going back to reading books for young children, which are just demeaning – they simultaneously need a challenge and a gradient on which to progress. The individual is the only person who will know what they might be interested in reading and when that will be. Individuals _can_ teach themselves to read, which leaves them free to pick their own time, place and reading material; for teenage boys for example, the sports pages of the tabloid newspaper often prove to be quite motivational. In our experience, motivation is much more important than the content.

To clarify your motivation, ask yourself "what do I want?" and then ask "what would that do for me?" And ask yourself again and again "what would _that_ do for me?" until the answer lands somewhere that _you_ are clearly very motivated to achieve. Once you get focused on what benefits it might bring, entertaining the possibility of change is much easier.

Always look for something positive you will achieve, rather than something negative you want to avoid.

For example

Q: What do YOU want?
A: To improve my reading and spelling

Q: What would that do for YOU?
A: I would understand more

Q: What would that do for YOU?
A: I would learn quicker

Q: What would that do for YOU?
A: I'd pass my tests in school

Q: What would that do for YOU?
A: I would enjoy school more

Q: What would that do for YOU?
A: I would be happier

Now this really is worth striving for!

How will you know when you've got it?

How do great spellers just do it?

> What are the captions or key words you would use to describe this picture?
>
> ....
> ....
> ....
> ....

When individuals learn spellings for regular tests, some find it easy, some hard, and some find it virtually impossible.

The good news is that we are not going to teach you any more rules, in this book. The English language is already a minefield of rules, counter rules and dreadful rhymes to help us remember. So we are not introducing more.

We will help you get in touch with the way your mind is designed to work and make full use of the skills you already have. You will learn the process with very simple words first; when you have the skill for simple words, longer words will follow without difficulty.

So what is the difference that makes the difference? 'Visualisation' is the process of capturing and holding a mental image or photograph and it is the way the best spellers spell, in any language. Being able to spell words by copying them down from a visual image is easy. You will learn to link this image to what the word sounds like and whether it feels right.

At the same time as you learn to read you also learn to spell, but some people find reading is far easier than spelling.   The essential processes of 'Visualisation', that can help with these basic skills, are rarely formally taught. They are taken for granted. We have often heard "well can't everyone do that?"

There are five simple steps, to the process of 'Visual Spelling' and you can do them on your own, or with a parent, friend or teacher - any time, any place. The steps simply build on one another. We have taken the process which all good spellers use and slowed it down to enable you to learn it. Once you are confident with the steps you will be able to run them at normal speed just like they do. As with any skill, practise makes perfect, and, with a positive approach, it is amazing how quickly individuals adopt this new learning.

Those people you speak to, who find spelling and reading really easy, may believe they do not use 'Visual Spelling' but the reality is they probably do, but it is in their subconscious mind, where it is completed so quickly that they do not even realise they have done it.

Part 2

Beliefs

What do you believe about your own spelling and reading? Do you believe you can improve or are you limiting yourself?

What is standing in your way to success?

What do you assume that limits what you do?

What do you believe about your abilities with words?

Your individual beliefs are very important because they direct the way you behave and the progress you can make.

For instance, what do you believe about your spelling? If you believe that you are a dreadful speller, you will probably be right and continue to be so; we all like to be right. On the other hand, if you believe something like "if I learn **_how to_** spell by imagining, or 'Visualising', the words and letters I will do better" then you may be able to achieve this.

In this part we will help you to investigate what you think about your own capabilities and assist you to change these beliefs for success.

If you already believe in yourself, your true abilities, and that you will be able to spell and read by the end of this book, you will probably be right about that too.

Where does it come from?

Your beliefs come from events that you have experienced and your reactions to them. If you are told and encouraged often enough "you are really good at . . . ." then you have probably come to believe that you are good at …. The same can be true if you are told "you are rubbish at spelling"; you come to believe it. But remember this is someone else's belief about one of your abilities and it is not your belief about "who I am". If it was said by a person of authority, such as a teacher or parent, you may be even more likely to believe it and let it stick – but you don't always have to listen to them. Do you remember being told that how you dressed as a teenager was ridiculous – maybe your hair was dreadful, your skirt was too short, your school tie was a shambles, or your shoes were a state? You may have ignored these because you believed it was 'cool', and you didn't worry about others' opinions.

You can choose to reject others' opinions about you, so why not try this for spelling and reading too?

How does a belief affect you?

A belief that you are a bad speller leads some people to think that they are "a stupid person". We have seen this frequently, but is, in fact, being quite unfair on you, as spelling is only one behaviour or skill to be learnt.

It certainly doesn't equate to being stupid. In our experience it's quite often the contrary. The older you are, the more stubborn this belief is to shift as it becomes part of you – your identity, who I am – "I am stupid", but this book will show you that anything can be shifted, with a little open mindedness.

If a child came to you and said "I don't know how to tie my shoe laces" would you say "You are an idiot?" No, you would show them how to do it, how to succeed; it is simply a skill to learn after all. In the next few pages we shall show you how to 'explode' limiting beliefs and re-frame them into empowering beliefs that will lead you to success.

As your new beliefs free you, your behaviours will free you too.

Practice 1: Identify what beliefs are standing in your way of progress. Then turn to the next couple of pages and see how you can choose to 'explode' these and change them to empowering beliefs.

I think/believe:

I think/believe:

I think/believe:

I think/believe:

I think/believe:

I think/believe:

I think/believe:

I think/believe:

Re-framing to take a new perspective

How will you start to change?

You hold your beliefs very dearly and the first thing to realise is that you can often change them easily, if you are prepared to look at things differently. This section describes a number of ideas that you might like to use to re-frame your limiting beliefs into empowering beliefs.

Now that you have collected together your beliefs look and see which ones are limiting that you might want to change. Change can be easier than you think; it certainly wasn't that difficult for most of us to stop believing in Father Christmas!!

What is re-framing?

In this context, a frame is the way you think about something and what you pay attention to. What is in the frame you notice, and what is outside the frame you tend to ignore.

Only part of me thinks change is possible

As you ARE taking the time to read this book, there is a significant part of you that wants to improve. However you may be aware that there is another part of you which maintains it is impossible and can even try to sabotage your efforts.

Such dilemmas are common and very often signal a time for personal growth. Whenever you learn something new you will feel this challenge, whether it is learning to drive or abseiling down a mountain. However the part of you that believes change is possible is the one that bought this book.

Ask questions

The essence of re-framing is to ask yourself a few questions and see how fixed your old belief is and how freeing a new one can be. If you were told as a child that you would never be able to spell, ask yourself something like:

- "Well whose life is it anyway?"
- "Why should someone I haven't seen for many years still hold this power over me?"

- "Is 'never' too long a time?"
- "What happens if I just find/create a new technique that really works for me. Will I give it a go and see what happens?"
- "I have always wanted to prove that person wrong anyway!"
- "I can spell some words, just not all of them – yet!"

Deletions, generalisations and distortions

These are 3 areas, which are all quite natural, in which we tend to simplify and generate a belief that may not be true on closer inspection:

- Deletion – we leave information out, for example "I can't spell" needs the question "What exactly can't you spell?"
- Generalisation – we generalise from specific instances to broad claims, for example "I can't spell" needs the question "What never, nothing?" You are bound to be able to spell some words; congratulate yourself on these

first and then you can add to them.

- Distortion – concentrating on one thing and ignoring something else, for example "I can't spell" needs the question "Who says you can't spell?"

The reason for asking you to be very specific about what you can do, is that you believe your beliefs and if they are limiting they will limit what you can do.

Avoid genetics

Your beliefs may have been influenced by the fact that you thought this problem with words ran in families; are there any exceptions to this? If there is just one person who does not share the symptoms, ask yourself how did they do that? Is it really in our genes or is it that we have picked up an unconscious habit? Reading and writing skills may not be the same with pairs of identical twins. So if you think you have no hope, just try suspending that belief long enough to consider that there might be an alternative reason, that you are yet to discover. Perhaps you are the one in your family to 'break the mould'. Blaming spelling and reading problems on genetics does not help you and can be guaranteed to keep you stuck. Think about moving on and leaving genetics behind.

Are they still valid?

Say your beliefs out loud, notice how they sound, tell a friend, tell your family – tell yourself. Sometimes individuals burst out laughing at their own beliefs – a belief you have seems ridiculous when you say it out loud now, although it might have been very valid when you were a child. Are there things that you still need to believe or are they now out of date, past their "sell by date" and you can let them go?

Discussing your beliefs with a friend can be a very interesting experience as you hear them out loud and you get another person's view.

Gradient – take it step by step

If you are looking for big changes in your beliefs it may be useful to take it step by step up a gradient. For instance, if you believe you can't spell words with more than six letters, make sure you are really happy with 4 letters, then 5, then 6, then a few with 7 and so on until you have blown that

Imagine success

You can even launch yourself into the future and imagine what success will really look like.

"When I am able to spell and read, what else might I be able to do?"

"What will it be like when the letters stay still, clear, sharp and don't fade?"

"What will it be like if I can see in my mind the words I am trying to spell?" "I can just copy it down"

Your new empowering beliefs

Where your focus goes, your energy flows

Now that you have some ideas of re-framing and 'trying other perspectives', the options are limitless. Give yourself permission to enjoy different ideas and see what happens.

Write down in Practice 2 your new empowering beliefs.

Practice 2: My new empowering beliefs	
What are your empowering beliefs about your future ability to spell or read?	How can you practise your beliefs?

Now you have empowering beliefs about your capabilities and skills these are what you want to focus on, the very things you want to achieve.

For instance
"I will be able to read and spell like every one else"
"The more I read the quicker I will improve"

Take a look at your new empowering beliefs. What can you do to plant them in you? Are you ready and prepared to live with them and the freedom they could bring you? How will you benefit from keeping them?

When you have time, take a look at your new empowering beliefs and see if you can make them even better; let your imagination run riot.

Take on a positive belief, such as "I believe I will become good at spelling and reading". The more you say it the more you will believe it!

See how YOU have changed your beliefs and enjoy being in this new place, your happy spot, full of new opportunities.

Carry your new beliefs with you, read them through several times and just sit back in the chair and enjoy them. Take pleasure in the feelings you get from reading your new, empowering beliefs. These new beliefs about your reading and spelling may open all sorts of possibilities up to you. Take every opportunity to inwardly digest and install these possibilities and grow your happy spot.

Have FUN !
You've found your happy spot.

Part 3

'Visualisation'

Enhance your essential skill of 'Visualisation",
which everyone has. Then discover how to
use it for holding words; what we call 'Visual
Spelling'. Practise is the name of the game
here and if it challenges you, don't worry – all
will become clear in Part 4.

In the process you will improve your visual
memory.

Step One – Can you visualise?

You have within you the resources you need to achieve what you want - including those necessary to make the desired change

Visualisation is the key to successful spelling

Just imagine, for a moment, there is a really noisy motorbike speeding up the road towards you, its engine is roaring as it races by – what colour was it? This is simple visualisation.

This part of the book will improve your visual memory. Once you can visualise well, you will visualise words and spell them by simply copying them down or spelling them from your visual memory. Your reading will improve too, as you access your internal image that matches with the word you are reading.

This 'matching process' helps you to recognise words or parts of words as you read them or visualise a word you are trying to spell. Without this 'matching process' you are going to find it really difficult and words can be very 'bewildering'. To give another example, if we don't know what, say, half past two looks like on a clock, it is difficult to work out time from scratch on every occasion.

Quoting from Don Blackerby's most valuable book *Rediscover the Joy of Learning*, "To be able to visualise in rich detail, to be able to hold an image so steady you can copy from it, to be able to instantly access large amounts of information, is a skill so significantly valuable for succeeding in school."

As this is such a valuable skill it seems strange that it is not taught in school, but seemingly the majority of the population pick it up. In our experience, poor readers or spellers never realise they can and need to visualise. At the other extreme, one individual who can spell perfectly in several different languages, can visualise many of the great art masterpieces, and in fine detail, by simply recalling an image in front of him.

We will now explore how you can develop this skill.

Where is your visual field?

"In your visual imagery"

The power to visualise comes in different ways. You may see a vibrant picture in glorious technicolor, or you may have a feeling and not be quite able to see it. You may find it easier with your eyes shut or open.

Consistently good spellers are found to look up to access their visual imagery, or 'mind's eye,' to see most words. This was confirmed in early NLP research, by comparing the behaviours of good spellers with those who found it more difficult. It is easy for you to check, with people you know, who the good spellers are.

"In your feelings"

Those who have more difficulty are frequently observed looking down, perhaps trying to think of the word, but also having an emotional response, perhaps under pressure, thinking how awful they are at spelling.

"Auditory recall"

Others look to the side, probably listening to how a word sounds, or recalling a well practised rhyme.

So practise looking up, to see new possibilities.

Practice 3: Have you ever mislaid an object?

Try imagining exactly what it looked like, what surface it was on when you last saw it, etc. Get the clearest picture you can, perhaps looking up, and restart your search – are you any more successful? You often are.

Good spellers are mostly unaware of these eye movements as they are so quick and barely visible. With easy words, they sometimes do not even have to look to 'match' them visually. Some people who consider themselves to be very visual, who for example can imagine their next holiday clearly, say they cannot see clear images. It may be that they actually look at their images so quickly, that they feel they have not seen them at all.

When you are 'in your feelings' and not feeling happy, your reading and spelling will often be worse. Of course, looking down to a book is bound to encourage you to focus on your feelings. It is interesting to try reading when you are happy and looking forward or up to a book. See whether there is any difference for you.

As all the best spellers use visual recall, the rest of Part 2 is about helping you develop your ability to use your visual recall skill and then use it to visualise words.

The next thing to consider is where your pictures are. Are they inside your head or can you move them into an external field of vision, where they are easier to see in front of you? Try the next practice to make this clear.

Practice 4: Just think about a cat.

What type of cat comes to mind? What colour is it? What is it doing? Is it moving? Where is it? How big or close to you is it? Does your 'mind's eye' give you an internal picture of a cat inside your head, or do you have a momentary picture that you can see in your external field of vision? Don't expect pictures to be stable for more than a few seconds.

Now try this. Can you hang your picture on the wall in front of you? How big is the picture and how big is the cat in it? Does it fade? Is it in colour? Which way is the cat facing? Is it sharp or slightly out of focus? How near is it? How long does the image stay there? It is also worth considering whether it is better to locate your picture on a convenient surface or whether it is better to float it in the air. The choice is yours; you are looking for what works best for you, as a still picture somewhere in front of you.

Take time to check out what you do have, because that is fine for you and the way your memory system works. Like anything else, if you use your abilities and practise, over time these can change. Once you have an external visual image from your 'mind's eye', you can open up many new possibilities.

Think about what you can visualise

To see how well you can visualise, let's think of a 'series' of objects. This particular skill, of making pictures, develops more than our visual capabilities. It also increases our memory and ability to remember a number of different items, such as lists. In fact, it is the method used by great memory men and women to remember endless streams of facts and figures.

Just to warm up take 4 words at random - *cat, grass, fence, yellow.*

Can you picture a cat? (What colour is your cat?) And your cat is sitting on the grass, and around the grass is a fence, painted bright yellow. By making up the story see how easy it is to remember four items when you have connected or linked them together in a sequence we call a movie. Now run the movie a few times to make sure you can see all of them, keeping them in the same order.

Now try moving on to a longer list, recalling objects in the same order. Read it once, covering it over as you make your movie – and then see if you can repeat the series of items. You only have to connect one word to the next word, you don't have them all in the picture together.

Dog, Grass, Wardrobe, Cricket Bat, Hat, Jelly, Bucket, Spear, String, Shoes, Watch, Glass, Lemonade, Green.
Run through this a few times, and – yes!!

Congratulations, you know you can visualise – you have generated a 'series' of images and learnt a very valuable skill in the process.

It's a great skill and one you can impress your friends and family with as they give you a list to remember. And more importantly it further develops your ability to visualise and proves to you that you can trust and believe in your capability to make pictures in your 'mind's eye'.

What sort of things can you visualise?

From Ian Robertson's book *The Mind's Eye*, he describes two categories of imagery that we use, which individuals may develop differently.

Sometimes these are in balance, and sometimes one is much stronger than the other. We use the 'what' and the 'where'.

- Using the 'what' you can recall a stable picture, like a photograph, of your front door, for example.
- With the 'where' you don't have a static picture, but instead take a tour, or movie, of your house for example, looking around the rooms you have, where they lead to, where the cupboards are etc, etc.

Now, as we look at words, which is more useful for spelling? We need to use the 'what' strategy of a picture, for words. You don't want to take a walk around it, with the 'where' strategy, as this only encourages all those different perspectives, which lead to confusion and eventually 'bewildering', as you can see below.

Ronald Davis, in his book *The Gift of Dyslexia,* describes how those with dyslexic tendencies "can perceive things from more than one perspective and gain more information from these perceptions than other people".

How would you hold pictures in your memory?

It is really important you work out what works best for you. Try Practice 5 and then read what some of our students have found and perhaps repeat the practice.

Practice 5: What is best for you?

Think of an object and visualise it – take a photo of it in your 'mind's eye'. You can then try playing with your image; adjusting the size and distance from you, changing the colours, adjusting the brightness, etc, until you have the best place for you to see your image.

Is it easier to see your image with your eyes shut or open?   If your eyes are open, check out the best location for your image. If possible make it in front of you, slightly up and at a comfortable distance. Once you have found the best location keep it stationary.

Practise as much as you can – you don't need paper and pencil, just a little time to concentrate, perhaps on the bus, in the bath, or waiting in a queue.

So many different experiences

When asking David to imagine in his 'mind's eye' a cat, he immediately had a clear picture of a cat from the front, back, bottom, side etc. He may have been running the movie of the cat to look at it from the other side etc, or simply flipping the picture around, getting a cat facing one way and then another. It isn't surprising that when he used either strategy for reading, the letters would tend to jump around the paper.

Philip's experience was very different, he had dozens of cats in his 'mind's eye', which was very 'bewildering' - you need to agree with yourself to just focus on one.

Jason, one fourteen your old, picked up 'Visualisation' in just 15 minutes. On the front of his school file was a colour picture of his favourite Arsenal club football player. When we asked him to describe the picture we clearly saw him staring out of the classroom window into the distance (about two football pitches away) and squinting slightly. Asking him what was out there - he answered that he had no idea. But when prompted to bring it slowly nearer, he managed to put it on the window frame and could now see and describe it. Showing him and covering a different picture, he immediately recalled the scene, having easily positioned it on the window frame. His response was "wow, this is cool"

What can you use this skill for?

Now that you are successfully developing your ability to consciously visualise we will show you some of the things you can use it for, at the same time as improving your skill, with a little practise. You will soon realise just how valuable it is for reading, writing, spelling and all those skills mentioned at the beginning of Part 1.

If, after practise, you find it exceptionally difficult to visualise, you may have stumbled across the reason why you gave up on the idea, earlier in life. Now you know it has a very useful purpose, persevere for a little and see what you can achieve. You will find that this skill is invaluable and normally becomes clearer with a little practise.

Step Two - Building your picture like a jigsaw puzzle

The meaning of communication is the response it elicits. The visual memory or 'Visualisation' of reading is the communication you have with yourself

Do you remember words or images better?

The first reading books have only a few words and lots of pictures. These pictures help you to gain a better understanding of the story and clearly visualise events. They give a ready made picture to remind you of what the story is about. Some people believe the pictures are only there to help them guess the words. Think back to the stories you read, to yourself and your children. Do you remember the words, the images that you conjured up in your head, or the ones that were drawn on the page?

Were you ever told to make pictures of each paragraph you read to help you to remember a story?

As you grew up and progressed to increasingly 'difficult' books, pictures became less, there were more words, the print was smaller - all reflecting the idea that you fill in the gaps with your own 'mind's eye' pictures. But did anyone ever actually suggest you make your own pictures? Not in our experience.

A large proportion of children pick up this skill quite naturally and simply start seeing their own pictures. When you are very young you can recall the pictures you see drawn in the book. As you get older, you 'visualise' and remember the information you have read by creating your own 'mind's eye' pictures. You are then able to answer questions correctly by recalling these 'mind's eye' pictures – this is the key to your success in comprehension. Some children, however, do not make this connection on their own.

For older people who grew up with only a few books, or books with thousands of small words and no pictures, is it any wonder that they may struggle with the concept that making pictures has any value?

Here is a short practice to help you understand this concept.

Practice 6: To bring this alive for you, read the following short story, or preferably ask someone to read it to you, and see how to create your own picture. Also be aware of how your picture changes as you receive more information. This is like putting together a jigsaw puzzle, where the words just add to the picture. When you start you will not know what the story is about.

There were no cars on the big wide roads of the city centre,……. [think of that picture]

but the pavements were filling up with crowds, held back by bright tape, …………[adjust your picture to put crowds on the pavements]

people were just standing waiting expectantly, gently pressing to the front…….[adjust the crowd to standing still if you had them walking about]

some motorbikes could be seen in the distance … [add your version of the motorbikes in]

but they were coming quite slowly and behind them were a group of people …[slow your motorbikes down and add the group]

You could hear distant cheering and as the group got nearer you could see they were running …..[adjust your picture again]

You could even see people cheering as they leant out of the windows of the buildings in downtown Edmonton in Canada .....[adjust your picture again put the word Edmonton in so you can remember it – perhaps on a banner across the road. If you have been to Canada you can make it more real, if not just imagine]

It was the opening day of the World Athletics Championship in 2001 ... [how about putting up some flags from the lamp posts advertising World Athletics 2001]

As the athletes got nearer the crowd went frantic, as the Canadian runner sped past........[the Canadian flag has a red leaf on a white background, put that in your picture too]

There was every nationality - Ethiopians, Spanish, Greek, Americans, English .... [How can you remember some of the other nationalities?]

The group streamed past so quickly, surrounded by bikes and cars, and with an enormous cheer from the crowd. Then they were gone, away into the dusk of the city centre, with another 20 miles to the end of the marathon ....[Can you put the dusk into your picture, perhaps also including a 20 mile marker post on the side of the road. Can you recall the noise of the crowd?]

So this is how you build up your jigsaw picture, which may be quite different from the quiet street you started with and different to other people's pictures. It is great if you know the title first to help you when you want to recall the World Athletics Championships 2001, but what you will recall is the picture you have created, and a few key words in the picture.

The power of imagined pictures

Have you ever read a book or listened to a story tape and really enjoyed it, visualising several possible endings until the very final page? You then see the film and it is a disappointment. It may have left out pieces of the story, failed to convey all the intricacies of the plot, or the leading actor was short and blond instead of tall and dark as you imagined. Your feeling of disappointment is because the pictures you have conjured up in your head do not match the images in the film. And guess which ones you are happier with?

One child said, "I didn't like that film because it was much more violent than the pictures I had imagined from the book" – a clear mismatch with his internal image. Children who listen to books on tape, or who are good readers, are great at this imagery.

Step Three – Seeing words and pictures together

A 'rich' picture lasts longer in the memory

The technique, described in steps 3 and 4, has improved spelling and reading for hundreds of people, and we are grateful to the pioneers of NLP, whose ideas we have integrated.

Let's think back to a practice you did earlier in the book. In Practice 4 you were asked to think of a cat and visualise it, adjusting it until it was in the most comfortable place and really easy to see.

You are now going to learn how to paint words onto pictures and hence learn 'Visual Spelling'.

Practice 7: Painting on the letters

Take another look at your cat. Whilst holding this picture of your cat in your 'mind's eye', write 'cat' maybe on the side of its body. If you have a black cat you may like to use white letters. To check your visual memory, think of something else, for instance, cleaning your teeth. And now go back to the cat again, checking that the word 'cat' is still there. Is the side of the cat the best place for you to see the word? If you want to move it to another part of the body where it is more comfortable for you and easier to read, go ahead and do just that. It is really important you make it the most comfortable place for you.

Practise a few times and you will find this becoming easier. You are simply practising to remember a new picture of your cat. This can take a few tries – after all you have had your old picture of your cat for a very long time, and this is a new one with letters.

Once you have your picture of the cat complete with the spelling 'cat' read it backwards 'tac', recognising you are reading it in this way. Make sure you are seeing your picture with the word cat and that you are spelling the word backwards. Once again, practise this a few times until you are happy.

Always read words backwards, when you are learning the 'Visual Spelling' skill, to check you are truly visualising. Without visualising, reading backwards can be difficult, especially with longer words. Once you can spell it backwards (and only then), sound the whole word out WHILE looking at your internal image of the word, and feeling it is right. This hooks the sound and feel of the word to your picture. Spell it from left to right from your internal image.

If your visual images are weak, you may find yourself having to trust the letter that first comes to you. This is so often the right answer and once you can come to trust yourself, you will be surprised at how this can help your images clear.

Run this practice a few times using short 3-letter words that you already know, adjusting the lettering until it is as clear as it can be – the colour, the texture or the position etc. We have also found that even

the case, shape of the letters, etc can be significant. Whereas many people recommend using lower case letters, we have found that some people find that upper case is easier to read to start with. This may be because the letters are more distinctive, for example 'ACE' rather than 'ace'. It is also worth noting that cartoon books often use capital letters in speech bubbles that some people find easier to read.

It is helpful to repeat Practice 5 at this stage to make sure your image is as crisp and clear as possible. If you find you get stuck with specific letters, make them stand out, perhaps pink and flashing, to draw attention to the correct spelling.

To make changes, give yourself a gradient (a nice gentle slope upwards). It is much easier to improve with practise and some intermediate steps along the way.

Don't let your pride get in the way here, practise really easy words first (3 letters) until you have become confident of this new skill of 'Visual Spelling'. It is really important to do this process one step at a time.

Remember you are learning a new skill and all skills need practise, especially if you have been doing something completely different for the last 2-50 years.

It is always inspiring, to see someone who does something really well, but it can also feel too much of a challenge. Ideally having an example of someone who is just a little bit better is more valuable. Who knows when you might overtake them! An older sibling can often be very useful here.

Now take 4-letter words and repeat this process in exactly the same way, making sure that you spell your words backwards as well as forwards, from your visual image. The more you practise the easier, quicker and more confident you will become.

It is useful to have a number of 3, 4 and 5 letter words already printed on plain paper, one per page, so that you can take a snapshot of them in your 'mind's eye' and add the word to your own picture.

Alternatively, you can use the pictures and words in the Appendix 1, thus visualising the picture and the word together, and try adding your own colours, to personalise your image. It is best to use words that describe objects to start with, i.e. they have objects in your mind.

3 letters – boy, car, pot

4 letters - bird, star, drum, coat

5 letters - witch, santa, clown

As your confidence grows you will be able to move on to 6, 7, or 8 letter words with more syllables (see step four) and ones without pictures associated with them.

Setting a **gradient**, means you can progress

one step at a time – trying to jump straight to the top can provoke a fall.

It is a good idea to check again how your 'mind' pictures look now as they may need further adjustment, as we did in Practice 5, to get the clearest picture you can. Again think about colour, brightness, sharpness etc. Think about it as tuning in a TV channel and adjusting the controls to get the best reception possible. As you practise this technique, making adjustments will greatly assist you. If you practise, over time you will notice that looking up and slightly to the left if you are right handed (to the right if you are left handed), even momentarily, may be the easiest place from which to recall pictures. However start from where you are comfortable and progress at your own speed.

Once Jason realised he could visualise pictures, he then visualised a few simple words in the same place on the window frame and could read the letters. He had a very clear image, so clear in fact that when we asked him to read them backwards, it was easy. We checked their size, colour, and background colour. He was able to change these and improve his picture to make it as clear as possible. Jason's comment was immediate, "this is incredible" and within days his teachers at St. Luke's noticed his reading was improving; and not just the few words we had taught him, he had somehow generated pictures of others too. It seemed that at the unconscious level he had 'switched on a light bulb' which now integrated new words and his spelling and reading abilities continued to improve. His brain had just learnt the essential 'how to'.

One youngster, John, we worked with, visualised on the inside of his forehead. When asked to check out how convenient this was, he replied "not very!" After two fifteen minute sessions, I asked John if we could move his words onto the wall in front of where we were seated. At once he was able to do this but, in amazement, he looked at me and uttered, "the letters are backwards"; we had a brief discussion about moving them but they didn't want to. The following week when I returned and asked him what order the letters were in, they had magically turned round the right way. What an amazing organ our brain is! Since this time he has progressed to learning lots of words through 'Visual Spelling' and his whole level of school work at St. Luke's has generally improved. Now the only time his letters go backwards is when he is confronted by a new word he has never seen before. This is a little signal to him not to guess but to learn it.

I cannot imagine how confusing it must have been to see all the letters backwards. It doesn't seem at all surprising that he had stopped using his 'mind's eye' when he was a lot younger. It was all too jumbled, too confusing.

Non-visual words

One of the problem areas is with joining words, those small words that don't have a picture. When presented with a word you cannot perceive or visualise, such as 'and' or 'the', the 'picture making' process is stopped.

Individuals regularly say "but they have no meaning and they don't make any sense either". This is an accurate description and when you look into foreign languages they are often absent. If you learn speed reading, you nearly always miss out such words, as it isn't hard to get the sense of the sentence without them.

The interesting thing is words that throw people are individual to that person. Clients often dislike, 'when', 'where', 'what', 'how', 'and', 'the', 'any', 'where', 'see', 'who', 'why', 'sure' and many more. Olive struggled with spelling many words as a child but over the years gradually improved. A few words still haunted her until she came across 'Visual Spelling', e.g. 'their'. You will invariably have your own list. Ronald Davis has published a list of words that commonly cause problems in his book *The Gift of Dyslexia*. There are often a lot of these short words in sentences, further 'bewildering' you whilst you try to read. You can make up your own representation in your 'mind's eye', for such words. Daniel Corney, who is autistic, explained on a TV programme that he has made a visual representation for every number to 10,000, so it is feasible that you could make a visual representation of, for example, 'their' or other small words. 'Their' could perhaps conjure up 'their car', or simply a picture of the letters, giving an immediate visual representation.

Robert, a teenager, was having extreme difficulty spelling and reading anything. We firstly checked whether he could remember anything visually. We asked him to draw this shape – there is nothing magical about it, it is simply an old Christmas card.

After his 1st and 2nd attempts he was then asked to trace it and feel the shape. His 3rd attempt was showing signs of remembering. His 4th and 5th attempts were making progress and remembering images. A week later we played a game with polystyrene letters and it became evident that he could recognise letters, even knowing which way round was correct. The following week we discovered he could spell 2 letter words. The week after it was 3 letter words. Using the cards in Appendix 1 he could visualise them on the wall. In 2 weeks he got up to words such as clown, santa, penguin and flowers. But he was spelling very, very slowly. When asked about this he said the letters were coming up one at a time. With a few changes he managed to get them faster and then all up together – but each letter was in a separate colour – what creativity. He was also reading much better.

1st attempt

2nd attempt

3rd attempt

4th attempt

5th attempt

Imagining 'where' instead of 'what'

When the 'what', the picture, is impossible with a word that has no visual representation, the 'where' strategy seems to be triggered, encouraging the 'mind's eye' to take a walk around the word, running the movie.

CAT
CAT
TAC

This is at best just a little confusing, and at other times it can be like putting fire with petrol – an explosion of overwhelming stimuli results in a 'bewildering' sensation. Adopting the same 'where' strategy continuously can generate numerous perspectives of the same 'word' at great speed, which may even make you feel quite sick. A talent, that is so valuable in other things, suddenly becomes almost a liability and can start messing up other programmes you are trying to run, such as concentration. This reaction prevents you from constructing a picture of the meaning of the paragraph (essential for memory) or thinking critically about something you are reading. How do you harness its power and stay with the 'what', which is essential for words, without drifting off into the 'where'?

If you experience a lot of words like this
that still really confuse you, take a look at
Part 4, "How to overcome 'bewildering' "
before returning here.

Hannah's 1st language was Hebrew, in
which she could read and write really well.
When she learnt English as a 2nd language
she struggled and was told she was
dyslexic. Now Hebrew goes from right to
left of the page, so at a young age she
would have been very comfortable looking
at words the other way around.

What are the captions or key words you would use to describe this picture, in relation to the skills you are learning? As you are doing this try adjusting the colour, sounds and feelings.

....
....
This is
like.......................................
....
....
because......................................
....

Step four - Focus on just the letters

Modelling excellence leads to excellence.

Now you have succeeded in remembering the words, and their spelling, by joining pictures and words together, it is possible to keep the image of the words and start to let your pictures fade. Start with the same three letter words as before, if that helps. As your confidence grows choose longer words. Write each word on a post-it and imagine taking a picture of the word, to put with the other pictures in your memory.

As you progress with longer words you may find it easier to split the words into syllables and create a picture for the letters of each syllable. Check out what works best for you.

Pain_ting   be_side   out_side   like_ly

Care_ful   yog_hurt   ball_oons   wall_pa_per

Or use:

painting   beside   outside   likely

careful   yoghurt   balloons   wallpaper

Practise is again the name of the game here, as you are installing a new way of doing things, so practise whenever and wherever you want. The sequence stays the same:

    a. First look at a few things around you - to get you into visualising mode. Now start with simple words.

    b. Write one word, per post-it, look at it and remember what it looks like – take a picture of the word in your 'mind's eye'. Look up and put it with all those pictures you have of memories or other words.

    c. Now recall it, see the word in your convenient place. If the word is long, you may prefer a picture of the letters of each syllable, and then put all the pictures together.

    d. Now from your internal image, see the word, and spell it BACKWARDS (from right to left) out loud; knowing you are deliberately reading it backwards. Do this several times. The only reason you are spelling it backwards is to ensure that you are reading it, not listening to the word or feeling it.

    e. Once you can spell it backwards (and

only then), sound the whole word out
WHILE looking at your internal image
of the word, and feeling it is right.
This hooks the sound and feel of the
word to your picture. Spell it from left
to right from your internal image.

Congratulations!! Well done on creating your
new skill.

Mary, an adult lady who did just one 40 minute
session, explained she had recently discovered she
was dyslexic through a special test at her technical
college. This made her feel better, "I don't have
to think I'm stupid any more, only that I have
difficulty spelling some words, and no trouble at all
reading."

When checking her eye movements, she was not
aware that she looked up when she was trying to
spell difficult words. When asked what she was
looking at she replied, "I haven't a clue." This was
great as she already had part of the 'Visual
Spelling' technique. After quickly teaching her to
visualise words, she knew what she had been
looking at and her spelling became far easier.

So often we meet individuals who read well and spell
poorly; teaching 'Visual Spelling' is then very easy
because they already know what words looks like.

Step five – Moving forwards with words

Sequences of words make a picture

In the same way that letters make up words, words make up sentences and sentences make up paragraphs, enabling us to communicate in written words with a wider group of people.

Paragraphs bring together a number of words, in sentences, until they paint a complete picture – this is the key to being able to remember the meaning of what we read. So try as you read a paragraph generating your own picture. As you read a sentence, notice what thoughts it triggers off in you, and hence increase your ability to remember the sense of what you are reading. For example, the lion roared and jumped at the school children.

Congratulations, your visual skills are improving all the time – you have now achieved progress in these 5-steps:

Step 1:   'Visualisation'

Step 2:   Building your picture like a jigsaw puzzle

Step 3: Can you see words and pictures together?

Step 4: Focus on just the letters

Step 5: Moving forwards with words

We recently helped a gentleman over retirement age, to visualise words. He reported in a two hour workshop, that he was instantly able to spell many words - he had simply learnt a new behaviour and his brain seemed a lot happier with the new habit.

Practice 7: It's a good idea at this stage to check what your images look like again.

Think of an apple and the word apple.

1. How clear is it? Could you make it clearer by adjusting the brightness, strength of the colours or sharpness of the apple and your letters?

2. Now look at where they are – could you make them clearer by adjusting their position - bringing them nearer (bigger) to you or moving them further away (smaller)?

3. Are they still (not moving) – if not what could you do to stabilise them?

There are many small adjustments you can make, so play around with your pictures and find out what really helps you.

Practice 8: Enjoy practising and see what stories you can make up to help you remember. Either write your own list, or use the list of items below - keep the same order:

House

Wood

Clock

Elephant

Tree

Waste bin

Earphones

Electricity

Shadow

Table

Door

Cat

Part 4

How to overcome 'bewildering'

Here you will help yourself through any 'bewildering' you may still have with words. You can gain new insights as to how your mind processes new things, and hopefully, eliminate this 'bewildering' with the 'EasyWords' Process. It will give you a new way to work with words.

What happens to you with words?

Try flipping the corner of the pages in this part and see the word Cat move around. This is a classic way for people who find letters moving around the page, to describe it to others - like children's 'flick books'.

Know yourself

Think about what happens when you struggle with words. Take a look at Appendix 2 that has some useful questions, to help you. What do you notice going on? Fill in some notes in Practice 9.

Pay attention to how words are written, what you find difficult and what is easier.

You will need someone to help you work with this part of the book and do take time to describe to them what happens for you; simply explaining to someone else how you currently achieve what you do, and hearing yourself say it, will be of help to you both.

Cat

Practice 9: What is going on for you?

Page 93

When individuals have thought about what seems to be going on they have reported comments like:

"I am searching in my brain to see if I have ever seen the word before"

"Everything goes blank"

"Letters are jumping around on the page"

"It's like one of those old 'flick books', where you see movement of characters on the page" (try flicking the corners of this part of the book to understand this and see what happens to the word 'cat')

"I don't want to look; the letters and the words are backwards"

"I can see some of the letters of the word and there are others flying around trying to push in on the act"

"I just ignore any punctuation marks, I don't understand them"

"Words like 'when', 'where', 'why' are impossible; they have no meaning"

"I feel quite sick and have to look away. The feeling comes on quickly and can take some time to fade away"

"I can read capitals, but lower case words get muddled"

What can others see?

Ask the person who is helping you to notice what you are doing; they don't need to tell you, but they will be able to use these signals to easily know whether you are still bewildering. Others can see your struggles at processing on your face – frowning, searching, squinting. You are normally aware of something, but often not these precise external signals, which are unconscious reactions. These are currently your automatic 'responses'.

Now you are beginning to understand what you are doing, you can look forward to building on what you already know, to develop the skills you want.

Later on you will have the opportunity to decide how you would like these to be once you have gained some more insights into how you currently work with words.

Invest some time to discover what is going on for you in completing Practice 9.

How do we learn a new skill?

"If we do the same thing we get the same results"

How do you learn new skills throughout life? How do you build your capability to master a skill and achieve something you want?

Do you remember learning to ride a bike and could you have done it simply by reading a book? We all pass through 4 stages of learning in every skill we have ever developed, described below as "The Pattern of learning":

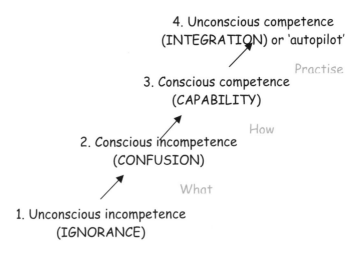

4. Unconscious competence (INTEGRATION) or 'autopilot'

Practise

3. Conscious competence (CAPABILITY)

How

2. Conscious incompetence (CONFUSION)

What

1. Unconscious incompetence (IGNORANCE)

Stage 1: Unconscious incompetence

We don't know we don't know

This is a state of ignorance: you don't know what you don't know!

Stage 2: Conscious incompetence

We know we don't know

The transition to this stage is to do with 'What?' You become aware of what you do not know in order to realise that there is something that you want to achieve. You know what you want, and you know that you don't know how to do it yet - there is a gap in your abilities.

Stage 3: Conscious competence

We know we know

The transition to this stage requires you to answer the question 'How?' You begin to examine the process of getting to your goal. This may be where we are now with learning to spell – you know your current capabilities and are looking forward to learning a new 'how to' based on the skill of 'Visualisation' you already have. You are able to do things, but you still have to think about what you do. As you develop your competence through practise you become more skilled, and eventually you reach the last stage

Stage 4: Unconscious competence

We don't know we know

You are able to do things skilfully, without needing to consciously pay attention to what you are doing. This is what we call the 'autopilot' stage, with the unconscious mind operating very quickly outside our conscious mind, just like any other skill we have perfected.

For example at the age of 2, we may not even know about driving cars (unconscious incompetence). When we learn to drive a car, we start off wondering what the 3 pedals by our feet are for (conscious incompetence). We "get some lessons, practise and pass a driving test" (building conscious competence), and then we "arrive at work not being able to remember the drive there" (unconscious competence).

We learn very early on to crawl, talk and walk. There are no manuals or workbooks for

learning these skills. Do you still think about how to walk? No, you are on 'autopilot', and walking is part of your subconscious.

Once we have perfected a skill, our 'autopilot' is running and it is very difficult to forget the skill again. Have you ever heard someone say "you never forget HOW to ride a bicycle or drive a car". This is because it is firmly embedded in your subconscious and without positive effort it is difficult to forget.

Our heart rate, breathing, sweating etc, are on 'autopilot', with us seemingly having no control over them in our conscious mind. In the same way, we can think in pictures very quickly, and often have a highly developed sense of intuition. These pictures pass so fast, we are often not aware of how we arrived at our conclusion.

Trying other perspectives

When you value the resources, you already possess, the door is open wide for more personal growth.

Doing the same thing gets the same results

If you continually do the same thing, without alteration, you get the same result. Trying the square brick in the round hole, again and again, you get the same result, get frustrated, distracted and eventually give up.

This section looks at the very specific skill of 'when confused, take another perspective', try something different and get a different result.

If what you are doing isn't working, try something else.

When confused, take another perspective

Have you ever considered just how good you are at trying other perspectives?

What do you do when you feel confused or stuck with a particular issue?

For our child persisting with the square brick in the round hole we will see the growing look of utter frustration as it just seems impossible until . . . . . they see the square hole, turn it and pop, in it goes - with utter delight. It made sense to look at the situation from different angles and try different ideas. Sooner or later their efforts were rewarded by the brick slipping into the right hole. With practise, this 'try something different, a fresh perspective' drops into our subconscious, operating on 'autopilot' as we develop a most valuable skill.

As you grow up, and meet challenges, you are encouraged to 'try another perspective', think positively and stop going around in circles. For instance, you can often look at things one way and then another:

- "I have just changed schools and miss all my friends" or "the new school has opportunities to do new things and meet new people".
- "Someone has annoyed me" or "I can see the other person's point of view".
- "I have just been made redundant from work" or "this is also an opportunity to start up that business I

have always wanted to do."

- "The children have just left home and I am naturally concerned about feeling lonely" or "new opportunities will open up to me that I didn't have before."
- "I am running a difficult and complex project and I can't see the next steps" or "what needs to happen to make great progress?"

Just like some other skills we learn, there is no manual for learning how to 'try another perspective'. It is just something you develop and may become very competent at. If you have developed this skill during the first few years of your life, you may have decided this is the thing to do when you are confused, just as having a drink is what you do when you are thirsty. So confusion may trigger you to check out other perspectives and it works well for so many different activities.

We should also remember that confusion is a natural function of the brain, which happens when you are learning. As you become proficient the confusion reduces. Using trial and error and learning from your experience is the key to success. When you learned to walk, you took a step, fell over and then you tried something different - taking another perspective. Eventually you got the result you wanted. However, if your skill doesn't improve you can become overwhelmed by stimuli or new surroundings, you need to take a break, assess and recover.

There is a great part of the GCSE maths syllabus which seems tailor made for people with these skills – it is called rotation, transposition, reflection. This spatial awareness requires you to manipulate shapes such as triangles, squares etc in your 'mind's eye' and present them on paper as new shapes. If you find this geometric maths simple, you are expert in manipulating your 'mind's eye', and seeing another perspective. Many people who struggle with reading and spelling find the spatial awareness easy. We have also met individuals who are great spellers and very poor at spatial awareness. You will see the reason for this later in this section.

Take a look at the picture. What do you see? (You will find the 'answer' at the end of this section)

In the next section, you will get insights into what happens when you are presented with too many choices and how this understanding can assist you.

Too many perspectives

Imagine now what would happen if you can see so many alternative possibilities, that you have no idea which one to choose and cannot make a decision – you feel bewildered. You typically give up and have to wait for someone else to make the decision. You are like the fox who is caught stuck in the car headlights – bewildered, frozen and unable to make a decision.

If, for example, you try to visualise a cat and you can see lots of different cats, all different colours and doing different things,

Cat

this is enough to overload anyone, especially a young child and leads to 'bewildering'.

Sometimes when children learn to talk, they can get so much assistance from helpful adults, they just give up for a time, 'bewildered', so they can do it at their own pace.

A certain level of confusion is good and a stage in our learning levels, see page 96. Normally it signals a breakthrough in understanding, triggering you to 'try different perspectives'. But, if none of the different perspectives work, too many choices leads to massive confusion, overwhelm and 'bewildering'.

> Barbara recalled being so confused at school with words she was told to sit and look out of the window. She developed the capability to redesign the playground in great detail and hold the whole picture in her 'mind's eye'. Not the sort of thing her teacher was interested in, but a great skill for a small child and very useful for an architect.

Just one of our skills on 'autopilot'

What was it like when you became an expert?

If you have learnt the skill well of "when I am confused, I find another perspective" at a young age this will be firmly on 'autopilot', running in your subconscious. So every time you find a confusing situation, you try something different until you get the desired result and it isn't surprising that with this skill you are noticed to be a bright child, being able to work things out, fit puzzles together and solve all the usual childhood games, which are often 3-dimensional.

By this time you have lots of other skills on "autopilot" too that you no longer have to think consciously how to achieve, for example, walking, running, focusing your eyes, etc.

When you first meet words it is around the time when you first go to school and you are confronted with an external rule book which is different and may be very daunting. You may be put under pressure by teachers, or simply put yourself under pressure to achieve a new skill with words.

When confronted with our first words and being naturally confused, your subconscious may come up with "I've got a solution for you". It tries different perspectives, completely on 'autopilot', and unknown to your conscious mind, like the 'where' strategy on page 59.

First you flip the image one way, then the other, looking at the back, the side, the top, the bottom etc. With words, trying out other perspectives just does not work.

This 'try another perspective' skill is simply the wrong tool for the job.

In the next section we will explain what this simple error can lead to and how to change the way you think about words as 2-dimensional fixed objects, rather than 3-dimensional objects that can be manipulated.

Remember the picture in this section? There are two answers – one is a rabbit and one is a duck – a famous drawing of the 'rabduck'. It all depends which perspective you take. If you look at this one way you may be able to see a duck, if you look at it another you may be able to see a rabbit.

Understanding 'bewildering'

How many of our thoughts are the same as yesterday's, and will still be the same tomorrow, unless we change our perspective?

'Bewildering', in this context, is the direct result of using this 'try another perspective' skill for words. You may want to refer to the glossary for detailed descriptions of the terms used in this section.

Something triggers your confusion, you 'try another perspective' many times, seeing a word from different angles etc until you are overwhelmed with too many choices, find yourself 'bewildering' and eventually going blank.

'Bewildering' is simply interference to you clearly learning the 'right strategy' for doing a new skill and has probably been built up over years of trying hard to succeed.

The particular 'bewildering' you have may depend on all sorts of triggers, the size of the words, whether or not they are in capitals, whether there are lots on the page without much spacing, the font used, the type of the word etc. This section will lift

the curtain on this 'bewildering' and start to enable you to understand how you can reduce and possibly eliminate it.

'Taking different perspectives' can account for how individuals swap pairs of letters and find smaller words more difficult as they tend to spin around; larger words have more stability, and it is normally the syllables or vowels (e.g. ae, ea, ie) that spin around.

The result is we are even more confused with our first words and if we continue like this we will end up 'bewildering'. In the absence of any rules people naturally make up their own. In the absence of any visual language rules, people create/imagine their own.

Three to six year olds who stumble with words, don't realise that trying a new perspective of flipping them around isn't going to help, and need to be asked what is troubling them? What is going on for them? We need to avoid jumping in with "what does this word say?" This puts immediate stress on them to perform. It would be so valuable for every primary school teacher and parent to understand the principles sketched out here and to check out what the child is actually doing with words, before flipping them around becomes another habit.

Eventually individuals, trying to read or spell a word, can generate hundreds or even thousands of different perspectives in seconds.

Some people, who find words 'bewildering', tell us it is genetic and there is nothing that can be done. But pre-school the very same children often seem quite bright, because they have learnt to sort things out for themselves with different perspectives. Behaviours run in families too, so it could also be a learnt behaviour passed between generations. If this is so, we can always learn a different behaviour.

So how do we learn the 'right strategy' for the task we are trying to learn?

Quite simply people, who generate large numbers of perspectives, will probably give up on the word quickly and move on. So they develop a strategy for quickly ignoring words, punctuation symbols, and mathematical notation, which get them 'bewildering'. But reading a sentence without punctuation, such as commas and speech

marks, spirals to even less understanding,
but it is more comfortable than 'bewildering'.

See how motionless the heron stays when
focused on fishing – from one perspective.

You can perfect this strategy, of 'try
another perspective' long before you
encounter words. The strategy works well
for some things, but however hard you 'try
another perspective' on words it isn't
successful and you can end up with some
startling experiences,
all of which have been
demonstrated by
clients:

> The strategies we develop
> are the best we can do at
> that time, to make sense of
> our experiences.

- "The letters and
  words are backwards" (and

interestingly that clients know this). Imagine flipping the image of a word around the other way, like changing the image of a cat from looking right to looking left; then it's easy.

- "The letters are jumping around" – because you quickly look at a word from different angles, like in a flick book. There are special exercise "Trayner glasses", with tiny perforations in plain black non-transparent lenses, to exercise your eyes. It is interesting what improvements people have made to their eyesight using these. When some people first look through them, the letters on the page jump around for a short time. A perfect demonstration of getting the wearer to take different perspectives through the perforated lenses.

- "Individual letters swap, or some of the groups of letters in a word turn around. For example 'ea' becomes 'ae' and 'b' becomes 'd', 'bread gets swapped into 'draeb'. This is easy when you are expert in flipping words or letters.

- Words get replaced with something similar – so if you are struggling to read 'their' you may think it is 'chair'. The words have nothing to do with each other but their shape is similar in the client's mind.

- In maths, individuals ignore symbols, such as + and –. Maths certainly makes no sense without symbols.

- A student's work is found half way through a book, or even upside down, never starting at the beginning of the book and working forward.

- Students feel really sick when looking at words, without pictures, such as 'when', 'where', 'why' and 'who'. The same thing happens with a number of symbols such as commas, speech marks etc. These are know as triggers. It is not surprising that individuals learn to skip such words and symbols and not see them at all.

- "It is difficult to keep your mind focused on the page", with so many other thought processes going on.

This 'bewildering' feeling has been described as frightening (felt in your stomach) or like losing one's bearings. In Ronald Davis' book,

The Gift of Dyslexia he describes this as 'disorientation', likening it "to feeling dizzy when we are spun around." It may take a few moments or much longer to get over whatever feeling you have, depending on the individual and the strength of the feeling. We are using the term 'bewildering' to describe this feeling.

So what happens when you come across a word that is 'bewildering'? In a sentence such as 'the son of the old man kicked the dinner of the dog', if 'the' and 'of' are both trigger words, they will cause a 'bewildering' feeling every time you meet them and you skip these words. The sentence now reads 'son old man kicked dinner dog'. The picture you are constructing in your 'mind's eye' may even go blank, to get you out of a feeling you don't like. This is a positive personal reaction to protect you from further 'bewildering', but it has a disastrous effect on your understanding and hence your ability to recall or do any comprehension test.

Next we investigate how you can disconnect the link that this 'autopilot' has connected.

Breaking the link

What would it be like if you no longer had this reaction?

The challenge is to control when we take a picture (the 'what' of two-dimensional things such as words and telling the time) and when we run a movie (the valuable 'where' skill of looking at things from different perspectives). A written word does not benefit from being run as a movie at great speed, with the word moving so you see it sideways, from the top, from the bottom, from the back of the paper, etc, as if it is three-dimensional.

It's like when we are young and having decided we want to move, we developed the skill to walk. But if we jump in a swimming pool walking won't be great, and learning to swim would be a better idea. So we break the link with walking when we are in water, but keep it for walking on dry land.

We need control over when to use a picture and when to run a movie.

It is probably true that nobody asks you, or in many cases knows, what was going on when you first struggled. Even if you can logically understand the issue, how do you do something about consciously taking a photo, when your other than conscious thought processes are on 'autopilot', trying to run a movie?

One client used a 'working out words' technique to spell. He used a dialogue in his head, such as "the word bat is like cat and take off the 'c' and add a 'b' ", every time he wanted to spell a word. We can only imagine how much effort went into every written word and how tired it made him feel.

How can you be selective? Can you capture a manual override to use when you are reading and writing? If you can, hey presto your 'bewildering' could reduce and you would be free to learn to read and write <u>from one perspective only</u>.

Background to the 'EasyWords' Process

If it doesn't work, how can you change it?

The 'EasyWords' Process we have developed allows you to re-train your 'try another perspective' movie strategy that is on 'autopilot', irrespective of whether you developed it yourself or you believe it came from the genes you inherited.

You will need assistance to help you through this new learning process. A friend who can read and wants to help will be quite sufficient. Alternatively we can recommend people who have completed our short training programme.

You will have the opportunity to experience the powerful 'EasyWords' Process to help you avoid 'bewildering' and learn to simply refer back to the EASY way you can read and write some words.

We are grateful to Suzi Smith, Tim Hallbom and Robert Dilks for their work in the field of NLP, and developing the counterexample process, to help people lose allergic reactions. Studying and modelling successful people, has enabled us to adapt it, for spelling and reading to develop the 'EasyWords' Process.

Now that you are becoming aware of what is happening, you can start to consider how you will be different, and begin to ignore the interference caused by 'bewildering'.

It is important to note that using your reaction to run a movie and 'see different perspectives' is simply the wrong strategy for words. When a person is stressed, fatigued or anxious this reaction can look more like a panic attack, offering thousands of different options and leaving the conscious brain overwhelmed and blanking out.

Allergic, inappropriate reactions often form when people are going though a shift, or transition, in identity due to circumstances in their lives. Common transition times are starting school, puberty, leaving home, getting married, and emotional crisis – anything that changes the way you are thinking about and relating to yourself as a person. These inappropriate reactions

sometimes change when you go through a further transition. However, using the 'EasyWords' Process can be far more effective in quickly enabling you to achieve the results you want.

When we watch children, at a very impressionable age, trying to read or spell they often get frustrated and angry. Their frustration comes about because they find difficulty achieving what they want and they keep trying the same inappropriate strategy. We all like to be right. A strategy which has helped us out of confusion perfectly well up to now, is now causing confusion when used on words. One individual said they recalled thinking "what are they trying to do to me? Talking is easy; this reading and spelling is meaningless".

Have you ever watched a baby trying to take their first steps? This is an 'all waking hours', 7 days a week self-learning experience for most of us. It is about trial and error and not being upset if we fall over or make a fool of ourselves. There is no handbook or anyone telling us exactly how our muscles, tendons, bones etc work together to take a step. There's no teacher –

our body simply has to work out all this for itself. Mistakes are a positive and integral part of our learning processes.

We ask you to think and look at things differently. This may need a little practise. After all you may have been years doing something one way – but trying it differently will be worth it.

What are the captions or key words you would use to describe this picture?

....

....

....

....

Making all words EASY

Can you be open minded to find EASE?

It is beneficial to read this chapter through first so you know what to expect, before running the 'EasyWords' Process, that uses building blocks identified earlier in Part 4, within an NLP structure. This section is written as a script for a friend who is helping you, but can equally be used for you asking yourself, with [ ] annotation to indicate specific actions or pauses. We have also included some examples to purely assist your understanding of what you are looking for; but make sure you come up with your own answers, those are the only ones that will work.

The approach is not intended to replace medical or psychotherapeutic interventions. It is recommended that you use it to augment and complement any other treatment you are receiving. If you are under the care of a health practitioner, share the process with that person. The developers of the process have helped many people to change their response when struggling to read or spell specific words, and other basic skills.   The resulting increase in self esteem is often been dramatic.

Pre-work: Before this session, you must have completed Practice 9. This provides some form of check, to give you a starting point, to know how your response becomes different afterwards.

Firstly let us set intent for what you hope to achieve. If we make it clear what we are looking for we are more likely to achieve it. Say out loud something like: "I intend to follow the process as accurately as I can and be open to the changes that I may be able to make".

Stage 1: Your starting point

Standing near a wall on your dominant side (i.e. on the right for right-handers) mark where you are standing with a post-it on the floor. Take one step backwards, as you let a clear plastic shield appear in front of you. That imaginary shield goes from the ceiling to the floor and from wall to wall at the sides, so you are completely cut off from any 'bewildering' triggers, giving you complete protection.

Now see yourself, on the other side of the screen in the distance, faced with the word that triggers your 'bewildering'. You can notice the symptoms you have, but are not being affected by them.

Ask: **"As you watch yourself, notice how long it takes for the symptoms to occur. Is it quick or slow and what do you feel in your body?"**

[Keep a note of the answers that arise]

When you have the information from this step, let the image go, shake it off and let the triggers fade and finally take the clear plastic shield away, and step forward again onto the blank post-it.

Stage 2: What do you now know?

Think about what you now know about your 'bewildering'. It is just an inappropriate reaction to look at words from different perspectives, on 'autopilot' and outside of your conscious control. It is simply a mistake to try and understand 2-dimensional puzzles like letters and numbers on the page using a 3-dimensional skill. Mistakes happen, all you want is to learn from them, understand how to stabilise a picture and grow understanding of yourself.

What was going on in your life when this first happened? Perhaps it was when you first entered school and you desperately wanted to do the right thing to show your teacher or other children how clever you were. Entering school is a very important transition in who you are. Now that you know your triggers, you can make a different decision.

Ask: **"What would have helped make that transition easier? Imagine you had those resources then and notice what a difference it would have made. Knowing you have those resources now, what difference does it make now?"**

Stage 3: Benefits

This may sound like an odd question but are there any benefits to you from having this 'bewildering' reaction to words or spelling? For example, if you are coming up to exams, and given extra time to answer a paper, what difference would it make if you did not need this extra time?

Ask: "If you have had this as long as you can remember, does it feel like part of you and, if so, why would you want to lose it? Does any part of you have any objections to you having a more appropriate response to your triggers? Do you get anything positive out of keeping your current reaction? Would anything be missing or lost if you no longer had this 'bewildering' feeling?"

Pay attention to any pictures, words or feelings that come up when you ask these questions.

If you have any objections, ask **"What would need to occur for you to satisfy these objections?"**

Take time to negotiate with yourself about anything that surfaces here. You may need to decide how else you can get this benefit. Changes are easier once you have worked out 'how to' deal with them in your mind.

Stage 4: What do you want?

Ask: "How would your life be different now if you were not limited by this reaction? What would you like? What would that look like, feel like, sound like, taste like and smell like? What would that do for you?"

For instance, here are some ideas to get you thinking forward, but do identify what would work for you:

- "I want to be able to retain two-dimensions when reading and writing".
- "I want to be able to hold that steady state and look at a word as a picture from a single place".
- "I want to be present, here and now (not swimming around in previous criticism or future 'bewildering') and blocking out of my mind whatever else is going on".
- "I want to have control over my reactions".

[Wait long enough to formulate what you want and ask questions to make sure you are clear, about exactly what that is]

Stage 5: Finding 'EasyWords'

Construct a list of words that you are really comfortable with. These typically have pictures associated with them, such as cat,

dog, chicken, red, wall, your name etc. Do not include any you hesitate over, these need to be your best ones. We will use these resources to re-educate your 'autopilot'.

Take as long as you like to find the appropriate 'EasyWords'. These are the words that are not 'bewildering'. They may be similar to those that you find difficult but there is something about these that you never feel 'bewildering'. Remember at that time how you managed to read or write well, so you were having an appropriate response and it seemed EASY. Feel EASY now.

Write your 'EasyWords' on post-its and put them on the wall, slightly above eye level, where you can easily touch them.

Stage 6: Anchoring 'EasyWords'

You are now ready to start anchoring 'EasyWords'. You are looking for a state of EASE, when you are not 'bewildering'.

With your writing hand on your 'EasyWords' on the wall, and standing on the blank post-it, put yourself fully in the experience, remember the EASE when you think/visualise the 'EasyWords'. Fully experience these in your body and with all of your senses.

Ask: **"What do you see, hear, feel (smell or taste) as you are experiencing these 'EasyWords'?"**

For example, you may notice something physical such as the colour(s), shape, size, texture, stability, case or background of the letters. Also be aware of how your body is feeling – comfortable, relaxed, easy, confident .... What do you notice for you? These will be your resources for holding EASE.

[Note at least 3 in the box provided]

What are the 3 things you now notice about EASE?
....
....
....

Do this several times with different words on the wall, realising the EASE with which you are able to do this. Put your writing hand fully on the word, and press the thumb and middle finger of your non-writing hand, to anchor these positive feelings. An anchor makes it easier for you to recall a state; using your hand enables you to have a portable anchor

that can be recalled anywhere, anytime in the future. The more you practise the stronger it gets, just like learning any skill. Make your experience as real as possible. Excellent.

To test your anchor is firmly established, step away from the wall, take a break and think of something neutral like brushing your teeth this morning. Then stimulate or fire your anchor as you step back onto the postit, pressing your thumb and middle finger of your non-writing hand, and recall the experience of the 'EasyWords' coming back again, and the three dominant feelings of that experience, you noted in the box on the page before.

If this state is not EASY, take the time to re-do this step. You can repeat it adding more 'EasyWords', to strengthen your anchor.

Stage 7: Add an appropriate response

Now, in this anchored state of EASE, you are ready to add the resources.

Standing near a wall on your dominant side (i.e. on the right for right-handers) mark where you are standing with a post-it on the floor and take one step backwards, as you let a clear plastic shield appears in front of you.

See a picture of you over there, on the other side of the plastic shield with your 'EasyWords'. Firing your anchor, see yourself at EASE, enabling you to read these words easily. Again notice the 3 feelings you wrote in your box that are now so important about this state. You can tell by your posture and the way you feel that you have an appropriate reaction to these 'EasyWords' and you are the you, you want to be.

Now take your attention slightly to the side and still looking through the shield, and holding your resources, make a picture of you over there in the distance, looking at one of your triggers, but still having an EASY response and being the you, you want to be. Stay with the picture until you can see yourself having the same 'EasyWords' response to this trigger, and with any confusion dropping away as you adjust to this new skill.

And if you want to add any resources to help you go right ahead and do it - such as glue or nails to hold the letters down or look back to your picture of EASE, get support, fire the anchor and bring those resources forward again. Use whatever works for you, and stay with it until any 'bewildering' feelings settle down and you can view that situation with comfort and EASE. That's right.

Repeat this for other triggers until you know that you are retaining this sense of EASE, for all your old triggers.

Stage 8: Look how EASY it is here

Now in this anchored state of EASE let your pictures in the distance fade away and let the clear plastic shield go too. Imagine that at this moment you are in the presence of your old trigger, and enjoy knowing it is now one of your 'EasyWords'.

Take a look at the word, say the letters aloud, read it and spell it using your 'Visualisation'. If you have a word you don't know how to pronounce just spell it aloud.

When you can read comfortably all the word(s) or spell them aloud, that used to trigger you, give yourself a pat on the back, you have moved on.

Stage 9: In the future

How would it feel if you could suggest to yourself, in a friendly way, that you use this same response to other triggers you have ever struggled with in the past?

[Pause to allow as much time as you need for this]

Standing in the same space, imagine the next time when you are around a difficult word. Actually think of two or three different times when you can just put your fingers together and your response will be appropriate. Feel the EASE in your body and read or write the word. Excellent.

Imagine several future times when you have increasing control over how you react to reading or writing, perhaps flicking through a dictionary in your 'mind's eye' – EASY.

Stage 10: Test yourself.

Think about something neutral again. Now take a step back from where you started and you are ready to test. Without your anchor, think of being in the presence of the difficult words, and notice what your response is now, both in your thinking and in your body. Even though you may be expecting a repeat of the past you may be pleasantly surprised at how EASY it is for you now.

Think of yourself being with a word that used to be difficult. Notice a positive shift in your thinking as well as a shift in your response at this point. If that is not true yet, simply repeat the entire process from Stage 1 with the same or other 'EasyWords'.

If you need to, you can repeat this process as many times as you like for continued re-enforcement of your resources.

That's all there is to it. Congratulations on learning this powerful process. Enjoy your new response.

Having reviewed these stages, go through them for real from the beginning. Find a quiet spot, in a good sized room, where you can fully go through this experience without interruption and free of the telephone, TV, family and pets.

You may now have significantly changed your experience, and wish to repeat Part 3 – "Using 'Visualisation' to hold words". You may re-experience what this is like with your new resources.

Before you begin make sure that the friend, who is helping you, is familiar with the content of this book. Get a pen and paper, a pad of post-its for your spatial anchors and a felt pen for writing words. Organise an uninterrupted space and give yourselves time to make the improvements you want. Having taken care of all these preliminary requirements you are ready to start.

Change can be quick and lasting, observe progress, don't reject it.

The process is also available on a CD, and that enables you to run the process alone and have time to think for yourself, by simply pressing the pause button.

Part 5

The sky is the limit

Look ahead to what you can now achieve, with this new skill – the sky is the limit for you. Having cleared the interference you can now make way for learning. Techniques are included to help you to become a really fast reader now you have the basics in place.

What next?

What do you want to be able to achieve now?

You will notice things change – notice and value everything. Be careful, if you still think it is impossible to change, you may well change back again, as that is a very strong belief. Children are often very open to change; they only have to have a change suggested and they will be off, if it works better for them.

- You may suddenly be able to read words you couldn't before.

- You may be able to spell more words that you were only able to read before. It is as if you had separate reading and writing dictionaries and they have suddenly been connected. We have seen many students whose reading was good and completely unaligned with their writing skills. 'Visual Spelling' brings these two skills together.

- Try learning a foreign language and don't forget to use visualisation for spelling – now you can use it for your native language it will make a second language much easier.

- You may be able to better tell the time on a clock with hands (non-digital), as you can recall what various times look like.

- You may be able to remember number triangles (a modern technique used to multiply and divide, 2 multiplied by 5 = 10, 10 divided by 2 = 5 etc)

Of course anyone who is experiencing this level of change and improvement within themselves will dramatically increase their self-esteem.

Enjoy and celebrate the changes as you check out what is happening to you, and how much EASIER, happier and excited you feel around words.

Try taking 'notes by association'. When you listen to someone talking, do you tend to write down as much of what they say as possible, or are you practised in capturing your own thoughts? These are the thoughts that come to you as a result of what you hear. They will make very different notes, and will also be very personal to you. In months to come they will tend to have more meaning to you as they are your words and pictures, not someone else's.

Mind mapping offers an easy way to take notes or get information in and out of your brain, because they help you to work on paper in the way that your brain works. Mind mapping is great for coming up with new ideas, planning projects, taking notes etc. Mind mapping structures information with words, colours, lines and pictures. Students often find generating them great fun, especially as you get the opportunity to add pictures.

Tony Buzan has written several books on the subject, including a lovely one especially for children, which are referenced at the back of this book.

Eric has several difficulties including being deaf. He is a lovely lad with a real drive to learn. His teacher knew that Eric's spelling was good, but didn't really know how he managed this. Whenever he was asked to spell a word, Eric's eyes shot up and then he spelt it, without any hesitation. We worked with him in a group and we quickly found he was a self taught expert in 'Visual Spelling'. All we needed to do was to give him difficult enough words to keep his interest. We taught him by showing him the word, then asking him to write it down. We went through 10-12 words with him and then just gave him the first letter of any of these words and immediately his eyes shot up momentarily and then he wrote it down perfectly. We now need to use a dictionary to find enough difficult words for him.

Techniques for fast and exceptionally fast reading

How fast do you want to be able to read?

The first technique in learning how to be able to comfortably read aloud at a reasonable speed is to relax and just enjoy the story, hopefully building your own pictures as described in Part 3. The stress felt by some people in reading aloud significantly reduces their capabilities. Were you one of those children who cowered at the back of the class hoping the teacher would not see you? And if they did see you, would you have liked the ground beneath you to open up and consume you? The fear that trapped you was probably one of criticism and embarrassment, thinking how other students might laugh and how stupid you would appear. Olive carried this fear with her until her first child was born. She had always wanted to read the Winnie-the-Pooh stories. So this was her perfect opportunity to read aloud without criticism. Her son seemed to really enjoy being read to, or he just dozed off. Her confidence grew dramatically and the fear just dropped away.

Now you too have learnt this useful information about reading and spelling, and, hopefully dispatched your 'bewildering', your reading and spelling should be able to flourish.

When you have achieved some fluency in reading you may wish to see whether you can increase your speed. A lot of work has been done in recent years on the techniques of speed-reading, and this section will offer you some ideas and signposts for you where you can find more information.

With the help of Sue Blow, from the Mentor Group, who is accredited to teach speed-reading, the following summary has been produced.

It is easy to improve your reading skills; there are three main "crimes" which make reading slow and most individuals we work with probably do all of them:

- **Word by word fixation**: you read each word in turn giving each equal weight.
- **Sub-vocalisation**: when you are reading, you "say" each word in your

head as you read. This means that you will never be able to read faster than you can "say" the words in your head. Sometimes you can even see people's lips moving.

- **Regression:** your eyes flip back to earlier words.

You need to learn how to "bounce" the text, rather than moving smoothly down the page, trusting your peripheral vision to take in the rest of the words. With training and understanding most people are amazed at the improvements they can make in very short time frames. If you learn how to "fix" on key words and phrases forcing your pace down the page as you go, you will be amazed at how much you can take in, without reading, every word.

Understanding, when reading at speed can even increase. This normally stuns people, but can be proved with simple exercises. Compare the process to driving down a road at 20mph, you may feel dozy, concentrating on other things and distracted. And how many times have we heard people say this about those that struggle with reading?

Then think of driving down the motorway at 60mph. Most people are very focused and paying attention. If we use this analogy for reading, the faster we read, the less distracted we are and the more we take in. We find it easier to generate those all important 'mind's eye' pictures of what we have read to assist our memory; a win-win scenario. After all we can always slow down if we need to.

Tony Buzan has done much work on teaching people speed-reading in his book, The Speed Reading Book is in the Bibliography. Others have also developed fast reading techniques.

Depending on how much improvement you want, the sky is the limit. A change that starts slowly can often accelerate very quickly. Don't try too hard to make things happen, just notice and celebrate the changes.

Some other amazing facts about words

Did you know?

The following appeared as a mass e-mail to many people in 2005 and sparked a number of discussion web sites.

Don't ignore this because it looks weird. Believe it or not you can read it ....

I cdnuolt blveiee taht I cluod aulaclty uesdnatnrd waht I was rdanieg The phaonmneal pweor of the hmuan mnid Aoccdrnig to rscheearch taem at Cmabrigde Uinervtisy, it deosn't mttaer in waht oredr the ltteers in a wrod are, the olny iprmoatnt tihng is taht the frist and lsat ltteer be in the rghit pclae. The rset can be a taotl mses and you can sitll raed it wouthit a porbelm. Tihs is bcuseae the huamn mnid deos not raed ervey lteter by istlef, but the wrod as a wlohe. Such a cdonition is arppoiately cllaed Typoglycemia :)- Amzanig huh? Yaeh and yuo awlyas thought slpeling was ipmorantt.

Thanks to Cambridge University for giving us another perspective on how we actually process information.

++++++++++++++++++

Many people who struggle with words are not clear about whether they are right or left handed. Some individuals have compared their spelling with either hand and found differences and often believe that with one hand you write more from your conscious brain whilst with the other more from your subconscious. Writing quickly, and typically from your subconscious, without your conscious brain having time for 'bewildering' can be much more successful, once you have learn to trust yourself.

++++++++++++++++++

We may teach one of the speed reading techniques to some of our students at an early stage, as it is interesting that the very words that are 'bewildering', are the ones you tend to skip out when speed reading, they have little or no meaning, except joining sentences together. Touch typing is another interesting area for experimenting.

++++++++++++++++++

The age of telephone texting is now upon us, and it seems that teenagers have very happily worked out a new language that suits the way they think, using it to communicate very quickly. Whilst not suggesting it should be a new language, what can we learn about the ease with which they use it?

+++++++++++++++++++

Self awareness holds so many treasures for you achieving what you want. And the more you practise and develop what you have learnt in this book, the more you will achieve……

After all "Seeing Spells Achieving".

Glossary

Allergy: The physiological equivalent of a phobia, a rapid or repeated overreaction to a specific stimulus on the part of the immune system. An allergy is an inappropriate reaction to something that is not life threatening in itself.

Anchor: An anchor makes it easier for you to recall an event, a feeling, a picture, a sound or several at once. Music often gives you a great anchor for recalling past events.

'Autopilot': When you have become so competent at a skill, you have no longer any need to think about it consciously

Beliefs: What you take as true. The generalisations one makes about ourselves, others and the universe.

'Bewildering': The state of extreme confusion and overwhelm which can be quite unpleasant. Individuals describe it like coming off a fairground wheel, disorientated, fearful and having no idea what to do. It may result in physical feelings like sickness, headaches etc.

Confusion: A state you are in when you are struggling to achieve what you want. It is a natural feeling when we learn something new (conscious incompetence).

Conscious: Anything you are currently aware of.

Deletion: Missing out part of an experience when thinking or speaking about it.

Distortion: Changing an experience to make it different in some way.

'EasyWords': Alternative examples which you find EASY to read and spell. The 'EasyWords' are similar to trigger words but do not cause 'bewildering'. They are used to re-educate your 'autopilot' and produce new choices. They can be simple words or perhaps written in capitals. Whatever fits in your mind that you find EASY.

Framing: When you change the frame around a picture, let's say from brown to red, the picture can take on a different look or feel as other colours are highlighted. Framing is the way you label your experiences to give them meaning. Simply by changing the frame (re-framing) you can change the meaning of your experience and see things very differently.

Generalisation: A process whereby one experience comes to represent a whole group of experiences.

Going blank: A state that may be induced by extreme 'bewildering', and could be the body's way of saying "no more". A protection mechanism that diverts your conscious mind to think of something else.

'Mind's eye': The mental picture you paint of an object or word that you can see by recalling that image from your memory.

Overwhelm: A feeling of not being able to cope with too many diverse stimuli. You can't understand 'how to' get out of your confusion and achieve what you want, typically by continuing with the same thought patterns.

Re-framing: Changing your way of understanding a statement or behaviour to give it another meaning; changing the frame. The ability to reframe allows you to make meanings of events, that have previously been difficult or impossible, in ways that work for you and create desirable emotional states.

Resources: Anything you notice or need that will assist you to hold a state.

State: Simply how you are at any one time.

Spelling and reading: The process outlined is described for spelling and reading words, as these are the most common manifestations. It can also be used for reading music, telling the time, etc.

Strategy: The way you do something and the process you use time and again for doing it – some work well, but others do not.

Subconscious: Everything that is not in your current awareness.

Triggers: Words, numbers, punctuation, symbols, clocks - whatever starts the process of confusion, overwhelm and 'bewildering'......... A trigger can even be the way something is written, e.g. some people trigger on lower case letters or words and not on capitals.

Visualisation: The process of capturing and holding a mental image or photograph.

Your gift: This is the gift you have to run a movie, to 'see different perspectives' when confronted with a confusing situation. It is a valuable gift, a great strategy, the food of genius - you don't want to lose – for seeing other people's perspectives, solving problems, helping you avoid confusion, thinking things through in your head/'mind's eye' before acting and even solving jigsaw puzzles etc.

Appendix 1: Sheet of useful pictures

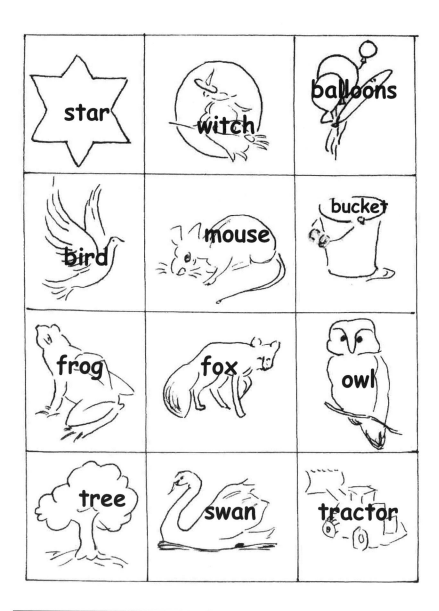

Appendix 2: What is it like being you?

The idea of this list is to help you focus on where you want to change and help you track movement towards those goals. Score yourself on a scale of 1 to 10 points. Do it before you start and again when you have been practicing a change.

0=easy, 10=difficult How easy:	score
1. Is telling your left from right hand?	
2. Is map reading or finding your way to a strange place 'bewildering'?	
3. Is reading aloud?	
4. Is reading for you?	
5. Is remembering the sense of what you read?	
6. Is reading long books?	
7. Is spelling words?	
8. Is reading your writing?	
9. Is speaking in public ?	
10. Are long words? Do all the sounds arrive in the right order?	
11. Are sums like in your head without using your fingers or paper?	
12. Is learning your multiplication tables?	
13. Is catching, kicking and throwing a	

ball like?	
14. Is doing jigsaw puzzles?	
15. Is clapping a simple rhythm like?	
16. Is it to see someone else's point of view	

Do you skip words when you are reading and if so which words?

Do you skip punctuation when you are reading?

What is happening within you when you try to do some of these difficult things? What are your thoughts and feelings?

What are you saying to yourself when you are working with words?

What would it be like if some of these things changed to being easier?

Bibliography and Resources

Barrington Stoke is an award-winning publisher that specialises exclusively in fiction and resources for reluctant, dyslexic, disenchanted and under-confident readers and their teachers.
http://www.barringtonstoke.co.uk/

Blackerby, Don A. *Rediscover the Joy of Learning*, Parker, Colorado, Success Skills Inc, 1996

The British Dyslexia web-page of successful people is http://www.bdadyslexia.org.uk/extra354.html

Buzan, Tony, *Mind Maps for Kids*, London, Thorsons, 2003

Buzan, Tony, *The Speed Reading book*, BBC books, 1971

Buzan, Tony *The Mind Map book*, BBC books

Davis, Ronald D. *The Gift of Dyslexia* Burlingame, California, Ability Workshop Press, 1994

Dilts, Robert. *Changing Beliefs*, Meta Publications, 1990

Dilts, Robert, Hallbom, Tim, and Smith, Suzi. *Beliefs: Pathways to Health and Well-being*, Metamorphous Press, 1990

Dilts, Robert Sections on Allergies, Counterexample and spelling strategies in his Encyclopedia of Systemic NLP www.nlpuniversitypress.com (available for free on-line).

Florance, Cheri *A Boy Beyond Reach*, UK, Simon & Schuster, 2004

Hemi-sync CDs and tapes are produced by the Munro Institute and can be ordered on-line from www.hemi-sync.com.

Holt, John *How Children Learn*, Harmondsworth, England, Penguin Books, 1970

If you are interested in the NLP Practitioner Programmes from International Training Seminars, Ian McDermott is quite exceptional. For information visit their website at www.itsnlp.com.

The Mentor Group, Ver House, London Road, Markyate, Hertfordshire, AL3 8JP. Tel: +44 1582-842077 www.mentorgroup.co.uk

Robertson, Ian. *The Mind's Eye*, Bantam Book, 2002

Russell, Ronald. Using the Whole Brain, Hampton Roads Publishing Company Inc, Norfolk, VA23502, 1993

Trayner glasses are available from Trayner Pinhole Glasses, Batcombe, Shepton Mallet, BA4 6BS, UK Telephone +441749-850822

Contacting the authors and NLP practitioners

You can contact the authors of this book through their web-sites:

Andrew can be contacted through
www.investinsideyourself.com
andrew@investinsideyourself.com

Olive can be contacted through
www.empoweringlearning.co.uk
olive@empoweringlearning.co.uk

If you need any help to achieve what is described in this book, you are welcome to contact us for assistance. We are also running training courses for those that wish to work with others. Dates are available on the web-sites. We will be able to provide details of those who have been trained in the techniques described here.

If there is anything traumatic about the way the belief was formed you may need to deal with this first. Traumas don't have to be life threatening. For example if you got the idea that you were a "bad person" because you could not read and haven't done since, then this belief may need to be shifted first. An NLP practitioner can help you to change this state using the NLP trauma process.

Index

feelings · 50, 54, 55, 68,
   71, 82, 84, 85, 94, 102,
   113, 114, 125, 128-131,
   147- 149, 154
flick · 92, 94, 112
Florance, Dr Cheri · 6, 24,
   157
framing · 40, 148
frustration · 16, 101, 119

G

generalisations · 42
genetics · 43
gift · 6, 5, 14, 26, 27, 60,
   77, 114, 151, 156
glossary · 108,147
going blank · 94, 108, 114,
   123, 127, 149
gradient · 30, 44, 72, 74

H

Hallbom, Tim 117, 156
Holt, John · 6, 29, 156

I

identity · 24, 38, 118
ignorance · 97

J

jigsaw · 64, 86, 150, 154

L

learning levels · 105
limiting beliefs · 8, 38,
   40, 147
lists · 26, 58, 77, 89, 126

M

manipulating objects · 103
McDermott, Ian · 5, 4,
   157
Mentor Group · 141, 157
mind mapping · 13, 17,
   138, 155
mind's eye · 4, 27, 51-90,
   103, 105, 114, 127, 132,
   143, 149
mission · 9
Morgan, Dr. Pringle · 26

N

NLP · 3, 54, 69, 117, 121,
   156, 158, 159, 164
non-visual words · 77

O

overwhelm · 105, 147,
   149, 150

P

perspectives · 5, 6, 8, 14, 26, 28, 48, 60, 80, 100-118, 109-118, 123, 150, 163-164
plastic shield · 123, 130, 131

R

re-framing · 41, 48, 149
resources · 20, 52, 100, 124, 127-130, 133, 134, 149, 155
rhymes · 32
Ronald Davis · 77, 113

S

self esteem · 3, 6, 23, 122, 137
state · 23, 24, 30, 37, 97, 126-131, 147, 149, 160, 164
strategy · 59, 62, 80, 107, 108, 110, 111, 117, 118, 119, 150

Smith, Suzi 117, 156
syllables · 74, 83, 84, 109
symbols · 22, 110, 113, 150

T

Trayner glasses · 112, 157
triggers · 86, 108, 113, 122-125, 130-132, 150

V

visual memory · 51, 52, 64, 70
Visual Spelling · 4, 15, 33, 34, 51, 69-90, 136
'Visualisation' · 15, 21, 28, 32, 33, 51-90, 97, 131, 133, 136

W

world athletics · 52

New perspectives

New Perspectives has brought together a unique set of books, especially for those who wish to explore how they can be more the person they want to be. The objective is to offer you, the capability to start your own personal development journey around the specific area that you are currently focused on, such as:

> ➤ deciding on and moving towards a new career
> ➤ coping with a recent promotion
> ➤ setting your goals and stepping up to the challenge
> ➤ losing anger
> ➤ wanting to feel you are doing a better job of being a parent, son or daughter
> ➤ recovery from illness
> ➤ moving on from a long standing health problem
> ➤ building your confidence
> ➤ reducing stress and letting go of what isn't important
> ➤ improving family and business relationships
> ➤ improving your skills to learn
> ➤ better communications with yourself and others.

Each book is focused on specific issues you may wish to address. If you find a particular book of value to an immediate need in your life you may become curious to understand more about other aspects. We would encourage you to move to other areas that you may feel appropriate.

The books are written by co-contributors, who are experts in this field or have firsthand experience of the material or topic being addressed. Some authors are Neurolinguistic Programming (NLP) Master Practitioners, with many years of experience of different aspects of personal development and professional coaching. The collaboration between the authors is crucial to the success of what they have achieved, and could not be done individually – an inspirational collaboration.

The books have many stories, examples, client experiences, pictures, dialogue and sometime workbook pages to fully illustrate the point and help the reader move forward. They will be challenging, as personal change can only be achieved if people are prepared to commit themselves to what they want to achieve.

As individuals grow within themselves they find that :
  ➢ Some of the day to day worries of modern living melt away
  ➢ Their focus on the things that are really important is increased
  ➢ A calmer and more grounded individual appears, less effected by any negative personal experiences, more able to cope with whatever life presents
  ➢ Energy and fun increase – often more than they ever thought possible
  ➢ Your inner wisdom shines through.